ROWAN WILLIAMS

An Introduction

ROWAN WILLIAMS

An Introduction

RUPERT SHORTT

MOREHOUSE PUBLISHING
A Continuum imprint
www.morehousepublishing.com

First North American Edition 2003
Morehouse Publishing
4775 Linglestown Road
Harrisburg, Pennsylvania 17112
www.morehousepublishing.com

Morehouse Publishing is a Continuum imprint

First published in the UK by Darton Longman and Todd Ltd 2003

A catalog record of this book is available from the Library of Congress

ISBN 0-8192-1990-8

Designed and produced by Sandie Boccacci
using QuarkXPress on an Apple PowerMac
Printed and bound in Great Britain by
The Bath Press, Bath

03 04 05 06 07 08 6 5 4 3 2 1

Contents

+━━>━<━+

List of Illustrations

＋＝＝＝＋

Preface

T HE INVITATION TO WRITE A BOOK on Rowan
Williams' theology for the general reader arose from a
profile of the Archbishop that I wrote in July 2002. I am grateful to my editor at the *Times Literary Supplement*, Peter Stothard,
for commissioning the article; to all my other colleagues, for
providing such an agreeable place in which to work over the
past few years; and to two of my former editors, John Whale
and Ferdinand Mount, who offered advice and encouragement
when my researches were under way.

Despite constantly burgeoning diary commitments, Dr
Williams himself was characteristically generous in granting
me several lengthy interviews throughout the project's
gestation. He has done much to guide an amateur like me
through new or unfamiliar territory. I am also indebted to his
wife, Jane Williams, and his staff at Lambeth Palace for their
charm and forbearance.

Almost all of the quoted material not referenced in my
footnotes comes either from unpublished lectures, or from
interviews with the friends and past or present colleagues of
the Archbishop who agreed to meet me. For the help they
rendered, I thank Donald Allchin, John Barton, Timothy
Brown, Gregory Cameron, Henry Chadwick, Richard Cross,
John Day, Hywel Francis MP, Anne and Mick Gawthrop,
Benedict Green CR, Bernard Green OSB, Dan Hardy, Simon
Holden CR, David Hope, Simon Jarvis, John Kennedy, Fergus

Kerr OP, Nicholas Lash, Ken Leech, Denys Lloyd, Gerard Loughlin, Sara Maitland, Alister McGrath, Chris Morgan, Densil Morgan, Richard Morgan, Oliver O'Donovan, Lynn Rose, Geoffrey Rowell, Chris Rowland, Mark Santer, Peter Sedgwick, Thomas Seville CR, Andrew Shanks, Eric Simmons CR, Cyprian Smith OSB, Angela Tilby, Denys Turner, John Walters, Brian Watchorn, Hywel Williams and Peter Woodman.

I am equally grateful for the practical support I received. Hazel Paling, secretary to the Bishop of Monmouth, handled my enquiries with good humour; Sarah Hillman typed up impeccable transcripts of addresses only available on cassette; Derek Jay provided otherwise unreachable material from the Jubilee Group archive; and the communities at the House of the Resurrection, Mirfield, and at Ampleforth Abbey welcomed me with great warmth during brief stays when the pressure of writing was heavy.

Six friends in particular have given me more than I can say. Glyn Paflin, Alison Shell, Arnold Hunt, David Martin, David L. Edwards and the late Colin Gunton saw early versions of the manuscript and suggested a great number of improvements. Naturally, none of them is responsible for the many imperfections that remain.

Almost twenty-five years ago, Rowan Williams ended the Preface to his first book, *The Wound of Knowledge*, by commenting that his problems had been 'immeasurably reduced by publishers as efficient, friendly and sympathetic as the staff of Darton, Longman and Todd'. Time has not eroded these standards. I have benefited enormously from the constant care and kindness of Brendan Walsh and his colleagues.

RUPERT SHORTT

London, May 2003

Introduction

ROWAN WILLIAMS' APPOINTMENT as Archbishop of Canterbury generated rare levels of delight and disapproval across the Anglican Communion. He was described both as orthodox and liberal, as a fluent communicator and impossibly obscure, as a diplomat and a dissident. Some observers spoke of his apparent ineligibility for the post. He was an academic who had not run a parish or an English diocese, at a time when most bishops are – and are expected to be – pastors and administrators. He did not come from the Evangelical wing (the strongest in the Church of England), at a time when many of its adherents regarded opposition to gay sex as a test case for doctrinal soundness. He was not a uniformly traditionalist Anglo-Catholic, being in favour of moves to allow women bishops. He took a stand against the looming conflict in Iraq, and had earlier described the Blair Government as 'obsessively interested in the manipulation of images, embarrassingly anxious about its portrayal in the media, easily seduced by the lure of big and vacuous words'.[1] For many others, though, these factors were deflected by a sense that he was head and shoulders above other candidates, as when a reluctant Churchill sent William Temple ('the only half crown article in a sixpenny bazaar') to Canterbury in 1942.

Williams' reputation for spiritual depth and academic flair extends back to his youth. He has also published three well-

1

received volumes of poetry. But if this makes him sound Olympian, it should be said at once that modesty and charm rank high among his other strengths. The shape of his theological talent tells much else about him: a keen intelligence is broadly channelled in several fields. His commitment to orthodoxy is complemented by a hope 'above all else that the years to come may see Christianity . . . able again to capture the imagination of our culture.'[2] This explains why he is hard to label. The tag of liberalism, in particular, is misplaced. True, he has shown supportive instincts towards clergy in same-sex relationships; but as the historian David L. Edwards remarked shortly before Williams' appointment, he is liberal 'only in the sense of being learnedly and thoughtfully honest and open'.[3] A representative list of his public preoccupations might include Welsh nationalism, the environment and opposition to abortion and the arms trade. He would prefer to be called a radical traditionalist – progressive on many social issues, glad to draw inspiration from the past, not coy about discriminating between quality and trash in the arts. A good deal of relativism strikes him as shallow or self-contradictory.

We are therefore likely to misunderstand the Archbishop without knowing about his *resistance* to liberalism in some of its manifestations. The Church of England of his youth was heavily influenced by a project traceable back to Schleiermacher (1768–1834), father of modern Protestant theology: that of adapting Christianity to the contemporary world. Williams had no qualms in principle about the urge to keep pace with the times, and remains sensitive to how much religious language can seem like pious projection to secular eyes. While aware of the noble instincts underlying much liberal theology, he also saw the risks associated with slimming doctrine down. Discipleship is (or should be) more than ethics tinged with emotion. Theology, as a response to revelation, is in no position to manipulate its object. The Church is not just a fellowship of like-minded people, but 'a gift created by God's act'.[4] As Williams later remarked apropos of the tension between two Roman Catholic giants, the existentialist Karl Rahner and the neo-orthodox Hans Urs von Balthasar, 'Christ may indeed answer our questions, but he also questions our answers.'

Does this make him a conservative, then? Not exactly. If his confidence in orthodoxy sets him apart from theologians engaged in so-called doctrinal criticism, he nevertheless lays more stress than some traditionalists on the way that Christianity is mediated through history and language. This accounts for his tireless warnings about facile certainty in religion. On the one hand, he concedes, theology makes claims about 'the context of the whole moral universe', and is therefore not likely at first sight 'to be content with pro-visional statements'.[5] On the other, religious talk deals with what supremely withstands the urge to finish and close what is being said. There is a rigour appropriate to theology, but it is the rigour of keeping watch over our constant tendency to claim the 'total perspective'.[6]

In other words, the discipline must be in some way self-subverting, given that its subject matter is by definition indescribable. Christians who are not chastened by the strictures of so-called negative or apophatic theology (looking beyond human categories to the God who cannot be conceptualised) have an obvious rejoinder – that God has broken the silence with his decisive utterances in Christ and the Holy Spirit. But the point is that such action takes shape in relation to the world – to that which is not God. A surprising amount of ostensibly orthodox language evades the conundrum prompted by this awareness, and appears to be based on the idea that God is simply an agent among other agents. It thus neglects a central strand in the tradition that it purports to uphold. Williams would want to point out that the mercy-seat was empty (Exodus 25:17 ff.), and that Christians walk by faith, not sight. He also draws support from Pseudo-Dionysius, the sixth-century mystic, who 'denies that, for example, the apparent ascription of number to the divine subsistents [realities] places those subsistents in any kind of set of objects. They are neither three nor one "in our sense of the words".'[7]

What is true in principle about the mediation of divine truth has in turn been borne out in history. Doctrine did not emerge in a vacuum: it was 'learned, negotiated, betrayed, inched forward, discerned and risked'.[8] The impact of Jesus' ministry was so momentous that the recasting of religious language took centuries to complete. In the case of incarnational doctrine, the process lasted until the Council of Nicaea in 325; and for Williams, a crucial insight is that those termed heretics at this gathering were essentially conservative in outlook (and arguably more faithful to the letter of Scripture), while greater originality and daring was displayed by those we call orthodox. He is not thereby suggesting that the Church betrayed the Gospels in framing the creeds. Against other commentators, Williams is clear that it was drawing out the full sense of what the New Testament contains in embryo. But doctrinal development was difficult as well as protracted. And if simple answers were not forthcoming over fundamentals like the incarnation, then we should hardly expect an easy consensus over questions such as sexuality and women's ministry in our own age.

What unsettles the Archbishop's critics above all, perhaps, is his inference that one may arrive at fresh conclusions via orthodox paths. He believes that the more contentious of his views are based on a quarrying of tradition to nourish contemporary debate – what French-speaking theologians call *ressourcement*. Moments of 'significant newness' in church history 'need to be understood as an uncovering of connections and resonances in our central doctrines that have never been "brought out in performance", as we might say'.[9] He finds the theatrical analogy helpful, pointing out that a good Shakespeare production may shake us up through its newness, 'but if it is really good it will make us say, "I never saw that," so that we go away from the theatre not thinking about a new and different play, but ready to read and ponder in a way that shows new depths in what we thought was familiar.'[10] This attitude is applauded by the novelist Sara Maitland, a close friend of Williams since the 1970s. 'He is just about the only person I know who uses orthodoxy as a challenge and not as a safety-valve,' she says.

So the Church sees through a glass darkly; but it sees none the less. These are the two components that Catholic Christianity seeks to hold in tension. Say too little, and you may betray the costly demands of the gospel. Say too much, and you risk sounding fanciful or authoritarian. Williams has been charged at one time or another with straying in either direction. Some people describe him as too positive about the Bible's historical authenticity, and given to utopianism in his vision of the Church. Louder complaints have come from those who think that in other respects he is not positive enough. This view is voiced not only by hard-line Evangelicals whose own language often looks simplistic to those outside their fold, but by some of the Archbishop's admirers and friends. One eminent Anglican academic withdrew an offer to review *On Christian Theology* (Blackwell, 2000), Williams' big collection of essays, through not being able to get a proper handle on its contents. 'The argument seemed to move from spiral to spiral,' he told me. Alister McGrath, a leading Evangelical, has applauded Williams' translation to Canterbury, but also complains of 'an unrelenting abstraction' in his work. Daniel Hardy, closer theologically to Williams than McGrath, is nevertheless blunter: 'All that groundwork doesn't yield too much on the ground.'

Anyone who stakes out a theological position is bound to prompt criticism of some kind. A perfect balance is probably impossible to achieve. One might note, however, that Williams is said to straddle the theological monocycle with assurance by many other experts, including a good number whose starting points differ significantly from his. At the beginning of *On Christian Theology* he distinguishes between three theological styles or registers – the 'celebratory', the 'communicative' and the 'critical'.[11] Celebratory theology is typically the language of hymnody and preaching. It seeks 'to draw out and display connections of thought and image so as to exhibit the fullest possible range of significance in the language used'. Communicative theology experiments 'with the rhetoric of its uncommitted environment'. Well-known examples of this approach include the appropriation of Platonism by the Church Fathers in the second and third centuries, of Aristotelianism by the Scholastics in the Middle Ages, and of feminism by contemporary theologians. Critical theology focuses on the awkward questions. It is alert to inner tensions and irresolutions. It asks whether there really is 'a stable conceptual area in the discourse of belief that will always remain unaffected by mediation in other idioms'. This approach may ultimately lead to agnosticism, or the 'atheous' theology of figures like Don Cupitt. It may prompt calls for a revision of dogmatic language, as seen in the work of Maurice Wiles and Gordon Kaufmann. Alternatively, Williams adds,

> it may move towards a rediscovery of the celebratory by hinting at the gratuitous mysteriousness of what theology deals with, the sense of a language trying unsuccessfully to keep up with a datum that is in excess of any foresight, any imagined comprehensive structure. And the cycle begins again.[12]

Two points emerge from this – that Williams' commitment to 'celebratory' theology is obvious from a reading of his works in the round; and that he does not consider this allegiance to be undermined by due recognition of the 'critical' mode.

An allied consideration involves his academic prose style, which even sympathetic readers find arduous, and at odds with the lightness of touch displayed in many of his sermons and addresses. Part of the complexity naturally relates to subject matter: Williams' scholarship involves a lot of heavy lifting. This is the view of Simon Holden, a Mirfield Father, who suggests that 'his material is difficult because he's taking you down paths you haven't travelled before.' Nicholas Lash, a former Cambridge colleague, agrees. 'If the result of Rowan's efforts is a certain lack of limpidity, that is no disgrace.' In any case, Williams has not produced a systematic work on doctrine, and probably does not wish to do so. *On Christian Theology* is an assortment of essays about fundamental themes. It was not written as a unified whole. We have already noted his aversion to the prefabricated language that holds so much sway across the religious and secular arenas, and the broad spread of his sympathies. 'Rowan is always very keen to do justice to all sides of an argument,' says another Mirfield theologian who knows him well. 'He tends to do this simultaneously rather than sequentially, and I think that explains the knotty character of his writing.' Non-specialists would be better advised to start with another collection, *Open to Judgement* (Darton, Longman and Todd, 1994), which originated in the pulpit.

Not only do his talks tend to be clearer, but it seems to me that many (especially when unscripted) are also bolder. And if form affects content in Williams' output, then an account of his thought that confined itself to written material alone would be flawed. It could even be argued that people who meet and hear him get a richer taste of Williams' ideas than those who only read him. In deference to this view I have relied on lecture notes from my student days, and on transcripts of other addresses that he has given more recently. The style of such material is in any case better suited to a general introduction of this kind.

What follows is a sketch, not a full portrait. But I hope that the quoted extracts above all, whether spoken or published, will help save it from excessive caricature. The emphasis is on reportage and analysis. Though especially interested in the Anglican and Roman Catholic Churches, I would not want to be regarded as a spokesman for either tradition. Chapter One gives a to-and-fro account of Williams' intellectual evolution against the background of his life. Subsequent chapters concentrate on four areas – philosophy, theology, spirituality and politics – in more detail. I have tried to keep the picture as clearly focused as possible, even though patches of it can only be seen from the corner of the eye.

Chapter One

STUDENT, SCHOLAR, PASTOR

ROWAN DOUGLAS WILLIAMS almost died not long after birth. The future Archbishop caught meningitis in February 1952, four months before his second birthday, and was thought lucky to have survived. He remained a sickly child, walking with a limp for a decade or so afterwards. The loss of hearing in his left ear was permanent. When the worst of the trouble subsided, doctors advised that his life should be made as easy as possible. Williams says that this placed a heavy burden on his parents, Delphine and Aneurin. 'He might have turned out spoilt, especially being an only child,' according to John Walters, a Swansea-based priest and lifelong friend. 'But the reverse was true. I think it helps explain Rowan's compassion.' The ordeal has stopped him from ever cycling or driving (but not from cultivating a fine singing voice), and accounts for something about Williams' posture. In conversation he habitually twists his head as an aid to hearing. This reinforces the sense that he listens well.

Aneurin Williams, an engineer employed by the Ministry of Works, was one generation away from the mines. His wife came from a farming background. At the beginning of the

1950s they lived in Ystradgynlais, a village at the top of the Swansea valley. Then as now, the area was heavily Welsh-speaking; in contrast to today, many upwardly mobile families chose to speak English. The Williamses were an example: Delphine, especially, had ambitions for Rowan, and one result was that he didn't acquire competent Welsh until his forties. Native speakers now describe his command of the language as impressive.

The family moved with Aneurin's job – to Cardiff in 1953, and back to Swansea seven years later. Their long-term home was a modest house in Oystermouth, a suburb on the western edge of the bay. At this point they belonged to the Presbyterian Church of Wales, but the allegiance wasn't unwavering. When their ten-year-old son came home one day asking if they could join the local Anglican congregation, Mr and Mrs Williams didn't object.

All Saints', Oystermouth, stands halfway up a hill with long views across Swansea and the surrounding sea. The original church (now the southern side of the building) was medieval; the nave and north aisle were added in the 1860s. A huge triptych depicting the Nativity dominates the interior, and the style of worship reflects a solid but not extravagant strain of Anglo-Catholicism. Going to sung Eucharists there must have astonished a child raised in the monochrome atmosphere of Calvinistic Methodism. John Walters draws a tongue-in-cheek parallel between the Williams family and the Russian envoys in eleventh-century Constantinople. Dazzled by the splendour of Byzantine worship, they instantly decided that Orthodoxy should become the new faith of the Slavs.

Aesthetics were only a part of the All Saints' experience. The schoolboy also fell under the spell of the Vicar, Eddie

Hughes, whose 34-year incumbency had begun in 1946. He was a man of rare quality. Rowan sang in the choir, served at Mass, and spent regular sessions discussing the faith with his guru. The years of illness (including lengthy spells off school) had given him an unusual amount of spare time, which he filled by voracious reading in fields such as history and folk-lore. This fed his appetite for knowledge. 'It must have been an extraordinary situation,' says Donald Allchin, one of Williams' later mentors, 'having this very bright boy knock-ing at the vicarage door and saying things like "I think I can understand so-and-so, but I'm not quite clear about the Trinity. Could you explain that to me please?"'

In 1961 Rowan won a place at Dynevor County Grammar School in central Swansea. His bond with John Walters was cemented by their shared dislike of sport. To begin with the two were forced to watch the other boys play football, despite not participating, but eventually they persuaded their teachers that they were better off left to their own devices. In Rowan's case these included music and poetry. He preferred polyphony to pop, and had read a lot of Dark Age Welsh verse, apart from more standard works, by the time he reached the sixth form. The child has proved to be the father of the man in other ways. On winning a prize for Latin in 1966 he spent his book token on Johan Huizinga's two-volume classic, *The Waning of the Middle Ages*. Soon before this, at the age of fifteen, he wrote an essay on St David for his school magazine. The piece disentangles historical and legendary strands connected with the saint, and includes this description of an abbey timetable:

> Later, after being ordained priest, he continued his studies under St Peulin or Paulinus (not to be confused

with the Roman monk who helped to convert Northumbria to Christianity in the next century), and then embarked on a preaching tour . . . The life in his monastery was noted for its harshness, and somewhat resembles life in a modern Trappist monastery; the monks, bearded, and with the front of their heads shaven, wore garments of coarse, undyed homespun, ate only bread and herbs, drank only water, and spent much of their time tilling the soil, using no oxen for ploughing but yoking themselves to the plough; candidates for admission had to wait outside the monastery for ten days to test their patience . . . Yet in spite of this severity, David himself was the kindest of men, and the monastery radiated that joy in loving God which was so characteristic of the Celtic monastic saints.

But the budding historian never seemed withdrawn or nerdish, Walters recalls. 'Rowan wouldn't have ended up as vice-captain of the school if he hadn't been popular. He also made his mark on the stage. I vividly remember him as the voice of the Washerwoman's Daughter in *Toad of Toad Hall*.' At sixteen, already endowed with his almost preternaturally deep tones, Williams won acclaim in the part of the Stage Manager in Thornton Wilder's *Our Town*. A reviewer commented on the challenge of the role (a kind of Greek Chorus), and praised him for his 'command, dignity and sincerity'. Two years on and by then the Dynevor magazine's editor, Williams was discoursing fluently and at some length on the subject of human rights:

Thus far, I have spoken little of man's duties: it is only too often forgotten that these must go hand in hand with rights. Many are prepared to talk much of their own rights, less about the rights of others, and hardly at all about their duties. We are, by the very fact of our existence, involved in humanity, and each individual is responsible to and for the rest of mankind. The great curse of the civilised world today is sheer selfishness, lack of concern and fear of 'involvement'; and therefore, I would in conclusion suggest that ... we should strive to promote not merely awareness of what human rights are, but also what they mean ... for in no other way will the Declaration of Human Rights ever become a reality for the world we live in.

Perhaps the gravity – and with it the implied optimism – stand out more at a distance of thirty-odd years. There seems to have been no doubt in the mind of the schoolboy that the path ahead consisted in prolonged engagement with the best that has been thought and said in the history of the world. This in turn would be shown forth in his life. Like other Christians, especially many Nonconformists, he saw an obvious link between Christian compassion and the rhetoric of the Left, and has been happy to call himself a socialist ever since. His reason for doing so ('I don't think the State is morally neutral; there needs to be an element of redistribution in policy') tends to look callow by comparison with his theology. Liberal Democrats and One Nation Tories could readily cite the same slogan in support of their own agendas. His political writings often have the same forthright quality.

But such debate, though vital, was not quite the heart of the matter. As a teenager he started to see everything against the horizon of his faith. The sense that religion imposes an intellectual straitjacket to be shed in the name of freedom had little or no parallel in Rowan Williams' experience. Surprisingly, perhaps, he felt continually stretched by Christianity, even when troubled by doubt. Nor did the process involve great feats of will. Struggle there certainly was, but also a willing surrender. Like almost every other believer, he knew more than he could say. If asked, though, he might have argued that only Christianity provides a language comprehensive enough to interpret everything else. The vocabulary concerned is simple as well as subtle. We are conscious and rational and self-determining. We are subject to metaphysical pulls, principally through moral obligation. Science can answer innumerable questions, but not those that matter most. The finite world points beyond itself. Reflection suggests that we are not self-created, and with the eye of faith we can recognise that God's nature has been projected on to the screen of history in the life of Christ.

Williams made other inferences besides. If Christianity were true, it would demand his all, including the relevant studies as a grounding for possible ordination. He applied to read theology at Cambridge, and was accepted before taking A levels in Latin, English and history.

+⟩━━⟨+

The university might have been made for him. Religion and high-mindedness were part of the fabric; revolution was everywhere else. Godliness and rebellion were not necessarily opposed, since many of the Church's grittiest critics came from the inside. The fresher went after a flock of new opportunities with relish, and Cambridge remained the setting for some of the happiest moments in his life. He has always preferred it to Oxford, his second English home.

Things didn't go all his way to start with. Stephen Sykes, Dean of St John's, his first-choice college, was away on sabbatical. Williams was interviewed by another don, who turned him down. At this point Christ's College stepped in with the offer of a scholarship. Christ's, a smaller place, was also less accommodating to theologians, and took only one student a year in the subject. But it had a vintage crop when Williams arrived: the other two undergraduates on his course, Christopher Rowland and John Day, are now both biblical scholars. Day says that Williams stood out almost at once as 'a saintly person, much preoccupied by social justice and helping the homeless'. When the tramps he met had nowhere else to go, Williams accommodated them in his college room.

Sara Maitland, an exact contemporary then embarking on an English degree at Oxford, fills out the picture of university life at the time.

> Many students were either left-wing or very left-wing. They generally divided into three groups. There were the Trots, people like Chris Hitchens and Tariq Ali; the hippies, of whom I was one; and the sober, duffle-coated types. Rowan was a duffle-coat.

Chris Rowland, another radical activist, soon became a friend. 'There was certainly great seriousness there, but it was diluted by humour,' he recalls.

> Rowan was extremely well liked, and always willing to have a go at something new. I remember him once

conducting a performance of a Mass setting by Rubbra in his second year. I don't suppose he'd ever done any conducting before, but it all worked well enough. Though preparing for Finals when he arrived, I was very struck by his intellect. He seemed to have read everything. After we'd known each other for about a year I met my future wife. Before introducing them I told her that he was the cleverest person I'd ever met.

So Williams already had an exceptionally well-furnished mind by the age of nineteen. As in Swansea, he was earnest but never really angular, spiritual but not priggish. Other friends noted an unmalicious sense of fun and a talent for mimicry. He soon made his mark in the Divinity School, where Geoffrey Lampe and Christopher Stead were among the leading lights. The person Williams revered above all was Donald MacKinnon, who taught philosophy of religion. This 'troubled genius'[1] held the Norris-Hulse chair of divinity from 1960 to 1978. Stories about his eccentricities abound: he sharpened pencils with a razor blade as he lectured, and sometimes gave supervisions from under a table. A set of talks on Hegel involved such a lengthy prolegomenon that the subject himself was not even mentioned until the final week of the course. The following that MacKinnon attracted was connected with his mixture of integrity and intensity. He had a more solid training in technical fields such as logic and epistemology than almost any other Anglican theologian in Britain, and a vivid sense of the challenge posed by philo-sophy to religion. But this awareness was yoked to firm Anglo-Catholic loyalties. MacKinnon's strong yet self-critical creed supplied Williams with the theme on which all his books have been variations — that faith has less to do with once-for-all answers than with a readiness to engage in further questioning.

Mark Santer, who once studied under MacKinnon and later taught in the same faculty, describes his former teacher as a far more substantial figure than Cambridge colleagues 'who tended to be either piously conservative or shallowly avant-garde'. This comment helps explain Williams' mixed feelings about the ferment then affecting the Church of England, and epitomised by the reception given to a book like Bishop John Robinson's *Honest to God* (SCM Press, 1963). Robinson was a respected (and in some ways highly conservative) New Testament scholar. Venturing outside his specialist field, he urged Christians to jettison a clutch of popular notions, such as that there is a 'superworld' of divine objects 'out there', and that Jesus was a supernatural visitant who made a space trip to earth. Instead, modern man come of age could identify God with 'ultimate reality'.

Some readers thought that this formed a healthy challenge to Christians and the uncommitted alike; others excoriated Robinson for undermining the faith of simple believers. Many non-theologians felt indebted to the author for giving voice to their problems and doubts. But *Honest to God*'s most sophisticated reviewers held that Robinson was merely restating established teaching in sometimes imprecise and ambiguous language. His argument that the Church had for too long pictured God as 'the highest person' or 'a particular thing' was a case in point: the traditional theology that Robinson supposed himself to be supplanting was also based on a rejection of this idea. As the Dominican philosopher Herbert McCabe argued, a very great deal of work has been done ... on the problem of how to speak of the existence of a God who is not a part of reality, who is neither a particular thing nor yet an 'abstraction', who is not any kind of thing at all and who cannot be defined or described. [*Honest to God*] contributes nothing towards the solution of these ancient problems but it does considerable service in reminding people that these problems exist.[2]

To jib at talk of the Word 'coming down from heaven' or 'the descent of the Spirit' was to show as much theological naïvety as to take such phrases literally, McCabe added. It might be thought helpful that someone could present traditional Christianity as something new, fresh and revolutionary,

> but in fact the air of iconoclasm which the author evokes has merely led to his being interpreted in a non-Christian sense. He has been hailed as an ally for the quaint evolution-worship of Julian Huxley, he has been widely regarded as substituting humanism for religion, and for this he cannot but blame himself.[3]

McCabe was also a potent prophet of *ressourcement*, and Williams learnt much from him and other Dominicans such as Cornelius Ernst and Fergus Kerr.

In the 1960s the Cambridge theological syllabus knew little of Catholic or Eastern Orthodox theology, and scarcely anything of how Christian thought evolved during the millennium between the Council of Chalcedon in 451 and the eve of the Reformation. Instead, students faced a heavy dose of biblical studies, much of it directed towards disentangling the Jesus of history from the Christ of faith. The experience can be harrowing. Christian students have to cope with the revelation that the text reveals both more and less than they imagined – more about its cloudy historical milieu and the tangled process of its composition; less about what it actually purports to tell us, given that so much of the narrative is mythological.

The discovery sometimes prompts extreme reactions. A recent fictional example comes in Alan Isler's novel *Clerical Errors*, where a priest educated in the 1950s and 60s loses his faith and asks, 'How can any rational creature not see in the story of Christ the pattern of countless pagan myths, the universal romance of the sacrificial god, his apotheosis and his rebirth?' But what counts as rational in New Testament studies is subject to change. By the 1980s and 90s it had again become respectable to express higher levels of confidence in the authenticity of the Gospels. In Britain the newer climate has been especially evident in the work of scholars such as Tom Wright, now Bishop of Durham, with whom Williams later collaborated in an Oxford seminar linking doctrinal construction with its historical foundations. Though written thirty years later, Williams' summary of Wright's book *Jesus and the Victory of God* (SPCK, 1997) draws together verdicts which both men had been feeling their way towards since student days:

> Jesus of Nazareth existed; he had ideas about his destiny and his place in God's plan; he had a coherent strategy, which the Synoptic Gospels accurately record . . . the early Church did not misunderstand him . . . The Gospels, again and again, make perfect sense in terms of proposals for the restoration of God's people – the

consummation of the return from exile, the reconciliation of outcasts and sufferers, liberation from the rule
of the 'nations', the Lord's decisive return to Zion and
the establishing of his authority there . . . What is distinctive in Jesus' mission is that he identifies the enemy
as inside as well as outside Israel: in the corruptions of
the Temple administration and in the collusion of the
mass of the people in something less than radical loyalty
to the Lord. Instead of just calling the people to judgement, he provokes a violent crisis, inviting his own
martyrdom . . . Yes, he considers himself the royal
Messiah, and, yes, his work is a political confrontation
with the colonial power and its local allies; but the victory sought must be God's alone, and thus the Messiah
must suffer, not conquer.[4]

Williams' difficulties with reductive approaches to the
Bible were not merely historical. As a believer contemplating
the priesthood, he was fortunate in being taught New
Testament by an Evangelical of the calibre of C. F. D. Moule.
The student's grasp of literary theory soon exceeded that of
his erstwhile teacher, but they could still make common
cause against atomistic approaches to Scripture. More sceptical voices at Cambridge were urging that the New Testament
world was both radically different from our own, and in-
comprehensible to us. This argument was logically suspect: it
claimed that we know what it assumed we do not know. It
also raised questions about the integrity of revelation. Though
not advocating a dismissal of historical-critical analysis,
Williams came to see that a doctrine of Scripture needed to
include consideration of God.

Again, words he wrote afterwards (this time showing a debt to the philosopher David Tracy) encapsulate his long-held convictions on the subject. The distinguishing element in reading Scripture 'is the conviction that it is a sacred text'.[5] And for Williams, a sacred text 'is one for which the context is more than the social-ideological matrix'. He admits that this cannot be proved by historical enquiry:

> It arises from a reading context that assumes a continuity between the world of the text and the world of the reader, and also assumes that reader and text are responding to a gift, an address or a summons not derived from the totality of the empirical environment.

Considerations of this kind form the basis of Williams' brand of critical realism. They have given him the means to recover an 'innocent' reading of the Bible at the far side of the interpretative experience, and explain his suggestion in another context that 'the simplicity of a Christian is the plaiting together into a single strand of all kinds of diversities.'[6] Fellow traditionalists express broad agreement with this approach. Critics think that the difficulties it purports to iron out are less tractable.

Williams took a First in Part One of the theological Tripos in 1969, and the top accolade, a starred First, in Finals two years later. It was clear that research would come next, especially as he favoured the then novel option of exploring Eastern theology. The Orthodox Churches had fascinated him ever since, as a teenager, he had been taken to see Swansea's

Russian congregation at worship. He applied to several universities, including Edinburgh and London, and says that he only ended up in Oxford because it was the first to say yes. The choice also secured him a highly congenial supervisor in Donald Allchin, doyen among Anglican devotees of Orthodoxy. At Christ Church, his home for the academic year 1971–2, and then at Wadham, Williams immersed himself in Russian religious thought. He made a study of first Sergei Bulgakov (1871–1944), Marxist turned priest, whose political writings he later translated, but eventually concentrated on Vladimir Lossky (1903–58), in part because this involved original research on unpublished lectures.

As at Cambridge, Williams became ever better at reading with high speed and comprehension, and didn't need to confine himself in libraries. There was still plenty more to life than study: services (he went often to weekday Eucharists at Christ Church Cathedral, as well as worshipping in Pusey House and his college chapel on a Sunday), society meetings, keeping up with a broad circle of friends. A discussion group brought him alongside three other traditionalists in the faculty – Geoffrey Rowell, Andrew Louth and Benedicta Ward – to devise answers to the challenges posed by theological liberalism. And there were practical tasks to get on with. He is naturally leary about rehearsing his own good deeds, but contemporaries remember his work with disadvantaged children in south London and elsewhere, as well as his perennial concern for the homeless.

It was in the 1970s that Williams saw his toughest trials in the laboratory of the spirit. The unfettered timetable of many postgraduate students in the humanities has a flipside in the opportunities for uninterrupted introspection. He knew about the risks of churning up one's insides, but not all his contemporaries had the same equanimity. He once said that he would have finished his DPhil a year sooner if several friends hadn't needed support through spells of clinical depression. The seductions of being leant on were also evident to him. Of two friends who met Williams at this time, one describes him as 'enormously warm yet radically private'; the other says he was 'acutely aware of the fragility within himself'.

Now that the prospect lay nearer, there was also much more soul-searching about whether to be ordained – and, if so, to which Church he should finally commit himself. His permanent adherence to Anglicanism was not settled until 1975 or 1976. Having left Noncomformity for a 'larger room', he sometimes wondered whether he might not become Orthodox or Roman Catholic on similar grounds, namely that the breadth of spirituality in these traditions could make the Church of England seem parochial. Donald Allchin had faced a similar dilemma in his youth, but was advised instead to 'be Orthodox in an Anglican form'. Williams also concluded that the insights of one tradition could be imported into another. That way, as he remarked, he wouldn't need to spend the rest of his life 'in intellectual and ethnic fancy dress'.

His attraction to Catholicism was tied up with the pull of the contemplative life, given that Anglican Benedictine houses are thin on the ground. He visited Downside (the monastery and school near Bath); but never thought about testing a vocation there. The place that really enchanted him was Quarr, an out-of-the-way abbey on the Isle of Wight. The timetable is based on a strict continental model (that of

Solesmes in Normandy): manual labour with some study, and
the seven monastic offices chanted in Latin, beginning with
Vigils at 5.30 a.m. He also came to revere a person – the
Prior, Joseph Warrilow – and later ranked him as his greatest
mentor beside Donald MacKinnon. In Warrilow's case, the
debt was more spiritual than intellectual. 'For all the harm
that celibacy can do,' Williams says, 'sometimes it opens
doors for someone to become wonderful. That was true of
Joe.' Having met Warrilow myself about fifteen years later, I
suspect that the magnetism had something to do with his
luminous joy.

As Angela Tilby, another old friend, has noted, the news
that Williams was thinking of becoming a monk opened
cracks in several women's hearts. Though personally
acquainted with the familiar tensions faced by *Guardian*-
reading children in *Telegraph*-reading families, he got on well
with his parents, and was concerned that they also were
hostile to the idea. Their sense of what counted as a successful career embraced academia, but not the literal life of the
cloister. He has retained a high esteem for the religious life,
but probably came to see his move in another direction as
part of a need to own desires that he once mistrusted too
readily. Those who knew Williams in his youth suggest that it
was marriage and fatherhood that finally helped this insight to
take root.

There were naturally theological reasons for his decision
to remain an Anglican. He admires the Catholic Church for
its seriousness, but has never been able to accept either papal
infallibility or the perceived authoritarianism that flows from
it. In the end, the Church of England's looser structures of
authority struck him as less exceptionable. As he said in an

early interview as Archbishop of Canterbury,

> For me, Anglicanism is a Church that has tried to find
> its unity less in a single structural pattern, or even a
> confession of faith, than in a pattern of preaching and
> ministering the sacramental action. The acts are what
> unifies it – the sacraments and the threefold ministry,
> and preaching the word ... If you are looking for a
> Christian identity that is dependent neither on a
> pyramidal view of authority nor on highly specific
> confessional statements, there's a lot to be said for
> Anglicanism.[7]

Establishment also troubled him less as time went by. It is
dubious to the extent that it confers special privileges, he
concluded, but defensible in so far as it rests on a presence
and commitment in every corner of the community.

Taking the habit might have cramped Williams' style in
other ways, given his political activism. He saw an obvious
theological rationale for joining the Campaign for Nuclear
Disarmament, drawn from just-war theory. Classically stated
by Thomas Aquinas, this teaching rests on the principle of
proportion. When violence is necessary to avert a greater
evil, it must be deployed within clear limits, and should not
involve the killing of innocent noncombatants. A nuclear conflict would entail colossal indiscriminate slaughter, and could
therefore never satisfy Aquinas' stipulation. Williams is
unimpressed by the main defence of deterrence (that it pre-
serves peace, since no potential combatant is reckless enough
to sanction mutually assured destruction or MAD), because
the policy involves the threat to kill innocent people in large
numbers. 'I know enough philosophy to see that a threat is a

provisional intention,' he once told a public meeting, before concluding that Christians could not accept a policy based on the readiness to perform unspeakably wicked acts.

In 1974 a group of Anglo-Catholic socialists decided to set up a support network, later christened the Jubilee Group, to counter the impression that there was nothing to their wing of the Church beyond a love of 'gin, lace and backbiting'. The move began with a letter circulated to friends and other contacts by Ken Leech, Rector of St Matthew's, Bethnal Green, in the East End of London, who described himself as 'very disturbed at the trend in the Catholic movement towards a sickly pietism and a right-wing stance in social and political issues'. He went on to say that 'this trend represents a serious betrayal of the social tradition of Anglo-Catholicism and it may spell the death-knell of the movement as such.' These remarks drew an avid response. Leech never intended to found an organisation, but before long he had a mailing list of several hundred names, and was planning seminars and a series of publications.

Williams, a founder member of the group, composed a manifesto with John Saward, a friend in Oxford. Later rejected as too triumphalist by other Jubilee members, this document begins with a quotation from the Russian theologian Nikolai Fyodorov: 'Our social programme is the dogma of the Holy Trinity.' It continues thus:

> We are committed to the struggle of justice, liberty and peace, not because of some secondary interest in social theory, but because of the very foundation of the Catholic Faith. We believe that man is made in the image of the Triune God, and is therefore social; that in

Christ he is restored to his full capacity for social being. We believe that man is called to share the life of the Holy Trinity, the life and love of communion. We cannot, therefore, feign neutrality, or remain uncritical, in the face of a society based upon the ruthless pursuit of private gain and unlimited consumption. The institutionalised egotism of all forms of capitalism, including the Soviet collectivised form, must be challenged by Catholic Christians, if we are to remain faithful to the whole Gospel of Christ.

It is unlikely that Williams would express himself in these terms today. But time has not softened the sentiment behind the tough talk.

⊷═⊶

His doctorate was entitled *The Theology of Vladimir Nikolaevich Lossky: An Exposition and Critique*. Russia at the end of the nineteenth century was undergoing unprecedented intellectual upheaval, as centuries of Western thought were telescoped into a few decades. Hegel stands out among German thinkers taken up in this context. His *Phenomenology of Spirit* portrays the human mind as rising from mere consciousness, through self-consciousness, reason, and on to religion and knowledge of the Absolute. Believing that the spirit of men and women is 'the candle of the Lord', Hegel held that we can penetrate beyond the world of appearances, and thereby break out of the constraints on knowledge laid down at the Enlightenment. As Williams summarises it, Russian theologians saw Hegel's position as offering 'a metaphysic of the world as organism, [an] intuitive account of knowledge and a certain relativisation of the ideas of an autonomous and finite ego'.[8]

Writing a generation or so later, Lossky detected philosophical dilettantism in constructions of this kind, complaining that they were insufficiently rooted in Eastern theology's primal data – the Bible and the Church Fathers. (Williams sees a Western parallel here with the revolt against liberal Protestantism by Karl Barth and his allies after the First World War.) Lossky's best-known work, *The Mystical Theology of the Eastern Church*, draws creatively on the negative way of Pseudo-Dionysius already mentioned. Apophaticism is not simply an impulse that can be qualified by positive statements about God: it is 'the primordial theological moment, the moment of stripping and renunciation'.[9] Theology begins

> in a kind of shock to, a paralysing of, the intellect – not by propositions that offend the intellect, but by an encounter with what cannot be mastered . . . the reality underpinning apophatic theology is 'ecstasy' – not a particular brand of individual mystical experience, but the sober acknowledgement that we must let go of the control of conceptual analysis when we are touched by God and advance to a stage beyond the life of conscious 'natural' individuality, closed upon itself.[10]

The result of this exchange is the experience of 'personal being', and for Lossky, human personhood emerges solely in 'the act of spiritual creativity which is response to the self-gift of God'.[11] The Christian vocation to personal being is underwritten by belief that Father, Son and Holy Spirit, being defined wholly by relations of love, gift and response, form the 'supreme paradigm' of the personal.

The thesis was submitted and accepted in the first half of
1975. But Williams still had no job. Deliverance came in the
summer of that year when John Walters introduced him to
Denys Lloyd, who then belonged to the Community of the
Resurrection. Founded by Charles Gore in 1892 and based at
Mirfield in West Yorkshire, the community has an eclectic
rule: members come and go more freely than monks, but
follow a timetable similar to that of an abbey or friary. The
Mirfield theological college is on an adjacent site, and Lloyd
got Williams an interview for a lectureship there. He was
taken on with a two-year contract straight away. Although he
was still unsure about the priesthood on arrival, his ordination in 1977 was made possible by this period of residency
under a college roof.

At its zenith between the wars, the community had
numbered more than 90 members. But by the mid-1970s it
was going through a wintry spell. The Superior, Hugh Bishop,
had resigned in vexed circumstances to set up home with
another man, and had made contentious statements about the
dispensability of doctrine. Several of his brethren also left,
and the noviciate was closed for two years. Williams became
close to several who remained, including Benedict Green,
then Vice-Principal of the college, and thus a close colleague.
'No one here had ever had such an exceptional range,' Green
recalls, instancing the new lecturer's grasp of languages,
history and biblical scholarship, as well as theology and
philosophy:

> Even in his mid-twenties, the analytic and the synthetic
> were in perfect balance. That is very rare. Rowan could
> have taught everything on the syllabus except liturgy

right from the start. I was constantly consulting him on matters of medieval thought. He seemed to have read virtually everything.

People again saw a mixture of warmth and reserve in him. 'There was a sombre side, a streak of residual Calvinism,' Green says. 'He was always gentle and kind, but the background colours were dark brown to black.' As we have seen, some of this came from empathy for needy friends (a number of whom were among a regular chain of weekend visitors). Some also derived from a broader sense of the tragic in life. A Mirfield Father who profited from his company speaks of the new arrival's 'tremendous and unfashionable stillness . . . but it wasn't the stillness of detachment. It was combined with sensitivity. He made me feel good. He made me feel that what I was giving was as important as what he was giving.' That Williams began writing poetry in a more concerted way at this time was also linked with his moments of dejection. Looking back on the 1970s, he mentions the novelist Susan Hill's comment that she has written most demandingly and deeply when unhappy.

This is borne out in Williams' longest published poem, 'Crossings'.[12] It consists of eight sonnets, the last of which confirms the developing impression that he is writing about an unconsummated love affair. The run-on lines lend an unforced feel to precisely crafted material, and the air of intimacy is sustained by a combination of candour and obliqueness:

So did we ever have an assignation
under the station clock? An intersection

of complicated routes? Was there a break
between connections when we might have snatched a
   word,
unusual and hard and timely, stirred
by urgencies too close for us to make
excuses, plead appointments for protection,
slew our eyes round, sketch a retreat formation
into the distance promised by the hiss
and echo of things setting to depart
all round? Eyes scattering far and anxious not to miss
something or anything; travelling apart.
You never came, we both of us could say,
angry, relieved, rejected, gone away.

His single biggest task besides teaching was the writing up
of his lectures for a book on spirituality from the New
Testament to St John of the Cross. The theme was appropriate, given Williams' conviction that theology originates in
worship, not in the seminar room. Published as *The Wound of
Knowledge* (Darton, Longman and Todd, 1979), it is a virtuoso
piece of writing, rich in insight and stylistic trills. The format
blends textual scholarship with practical insight into prayer –
part of the mixture Karl Barth had in mind when he spoke of
'irregular dogmatics'. The final page contains one of several
digests of the now well-known Williams creed, drawn from 1
Corinthians 2 ('I decided to know nothing among you except
Jesus Christ and him crucified . . . that your faith might not
rest in the wisdom of men but in the power of God').
Christianity begins in contradictions, he avows,

in the painful effort to live with the baffling diversity of

God's manifested life – law and gospel, judgement and
grace, the crucified Son crying to the Father. Christian
experience does not simply move from one level to the
next and stay there, but is drawn again and again to the
fruitful darkness of the cross . . . In the middle of fire
we are healed and restored – though never taken out of
it. [13]

The models of discipleship discussed include Paul, John,
Origen, Athanasius and the so-called Cappadocian Fathers
(Basil of Caesarea, Gregory of Nazianzus and Gregory of
Nyssa). Augustine – probably Williams' greatest intellectual
influence of all – receives full-bodied treatment in a section
called 'The Clamour of the Heart', some of which he later
summed up in an essay on doing theology. [14] Augustine
accepts that Jesus presents a new possibility in human
experience. But taking up his challenge to be born again does
not mean eliminating our identities. The Gospel says 'no' to
our fantasies and consoling images of ourselves, but 'yes' to
us as we fundamentally are,

creatures of God, objects of his love, called to fellowship with him . . . What happens in Jesus is new; yet, as
Paul and his followers constantly remind us, the hidden
truth of the faith is that it is also older than all human
struggle and drama. [15]

Like Plato, whose ideas he transposed into the Christian
key, Augustine was an 'illuminationist'. Unable to accept the
Aristotelian notion that sense experience is the fundamental
path to knowledge, he believed that our mental make-up
gives us access to a reality that transcends the physical. In the

Confessions he justifies this by arguing that humans, though subject to change, possess faculties such as judgement, that are not subject to change. The source of our powers of judgement therefore lies outside ourselves – with the God who summons his human creation into relationship. Traces of this intuition were common in European culture, at least as late as the nineteenth century, and Wordsworth's 'Lines Composed A Few Miles Above Tintern Abbey' is a familiar example in English:

> . . . And I have felt
> a presence that disturbs me with the joy
> of elevated thoughts; a sense sublime
> of something far more deeply interfused,
> whose dwelling is the light of setting suns . . .
> and in the mind of man.

Williams always wanted Augustine's echo to be heard more clearly in contemporary British theology. His hope bore fruit, albeit in a controversially bold form, with the rise of the Radical Orthodoxy movement during the 1990s. One of its leading figures, John Milbank, had been taught by Williams a decade earlier. By reinvoking the Platonic and Augustinian views of human reason as a participation in the divine mind, Milbank can argue that 'faith is not alien to reason, but its intensification . . . reason ascending is always grace ascending.'[16] This model also influenced the great Swiss theologian Hans Urs von Balthasar (1905–1988), whose colossal output has yet to be fully digested outside the German-speaking world. Williams translated several hundred pages of Balthasar's *Glory of the Lord* series during the early 1980s.

There were also applied matters such as women's ordination to reflect on. For years he had felt uncertain about the subject, but in the mid-1970s Williams' mind was made up when he started reading feminist theology at the suggestion of friends like Janet Morley and Pam Lunn. 'I remember his caution,' recalls Eric Simmons, then Superior of the Mirfield community:

> Rowan once gave a lecture in which he spelt out all the arguments in favour, and demolished them. Then he rehearsed all the arguments against, and demolished those as well. His audience were heavily split on the issue, and a number must have felt the ground shifting under them.

As professor and bishop, Williams would become strongly identified as a champion of the pro-women priests cause. Sometimes, especially in private, his tone could be mordant. Yet he always saw the injustice of portraying the debate as a clash between bigotry and the forces of light: traditionalist arguments deserved a serious hearing. The Church of England had done more to preserve its Catholic credentials than other Reformed traditions. Altering the form of the ministry in the face of pleas from Rome and the Orthodox Churches would harm the cause of ecumenism. In traditionalist eyes, this was a larger scandal than a male-only priesthood. For many outside the Church, of course, the status quo looked like an irrational and humiliating discrimination, and Williams was acutely sensitive to this. But he was also conscious of the bad arguments in favour of women priests – raiding the Egyptian storehouses of sociology, as he later put it. The case for change needed to be made with care.

On the ecumenical side, he concluded that to be Anglican is by definition to believe that there are circumstances in which gospel imperatives require unilateral action to break the visible unity of the Church. (The Vatican, in any case, was showing no sign of a willingness to rescind *Apostolicae Curae*, Leo XIII's 1896 condemnation of Anglican orders.) And opponents of women priests who complained that supporters were dancing to a secular tune could have this charge thrown back at them: church tradition contained too much disturbing material portraying women as defective human beings. Above all, Williams thought that the case for reform could be inferred from the incarnation itself. Patristic teaching on Jesus' attributes had been grounded in the claim that 'the unassumed is unhealed' — and what Christ 'assumed' was representative humanity, not only maleness. This argument would blow away the defence of a single-sex priesthood on the grounds that the apostles were men, Williams thought. They were also Jews; but no one had ever seriously claimed that Gentiles were thereby unfit to stand at the altar *in persona Christi*.

+—=—+

His colleagues took it for granted that bigger academic posts would be his for the taking in due course, and were unsurprised by his appointment to the staff at Westcott House (one of Cambridge's two Anglican theological colleges) in 1977. A similar sense that he was destined for a successively larger profile would lie behind his three subsequent appointments — as a university lecturer for six years from 1980; Fellow and Dean of Clare College, 1984–86; and Lady

Margaret Professor of Divinity at Oxford, 1986–92. The years that made up his second Cambridge phase were very productive. He published two books besides *The Wound of Knowledge*, and continued to attract the devotion of all sorts and conditions of people. In 1979 he had the fortune to meet Jane Paul, a postgraduate student working on the German theologian Jürgen Moltmann, and to achieve lasting happiness through their marriage two years later. (Friends say they knew that the courtship was serious, because 'Rowan had finally started to give his beard a regular comb.')

Ordained to the diaconate as soon as he returned to Cambridge, Williams became chaplain as well as tutor at Westcott, adding a pastoral string to his bow. There were many demands to be juggled. 'I'm not sure he was always that happy,' suggests the philosopher Andrew Shanks, a pupil at the time. 'There's often a hothouse atmosphere in most theological colleges – students are under a high degree of pressure. Rowan also had a lot to deal with, but he was outstanding both as a teacher and counsellor.' These sentiments are backed up by Mark Santer, then Principal of Westcott, who adds that neither administration nor 'bloodiness' – dealing with the inevitable conflicts with and between students – were among his younger colleague's strengths.

He was the toast of the divinity faculty. The Regius Professor, Geoffrey Lampe, called him the most exciting theological talent in Cambridge, and urged that he should be given a university position as soon as possible. Lampe died in 1979, but his wish was granted when Williams' lectureship was conferred a few months later. He felt eager to get some first-hand parish experience as well, and asked if he could become a part-time curate for Brian Watchorn, Vicar of St

George's, Chesterton, in the city's northern suburbs. Watchorn was glad of the offer, and Williams spent the next three years living in the curate's house on the Arbury council estate. Though his lectureship was a full-time job, he did as much as he could in the parish besides taking services, and was effectively in charge during a three-month interregnum in 1982.

Talents emerged that might have surprised some who had only seen his cerebral side. He ran a large and successful Sunday school, for example, and several onlookers remember his talent for preaching well to children. 'He produced beautiful, chiselled little homilies,' Watchorn says. 'Even if people found his adult sermons hard to understand, it didn't matter. They knew he was a holy man.' Mick Gawthrop, a baker, and his wife Anne were a mainstay of the St George's congregation during the Williamses' time there, and their friendship has lasted ever since. 'I've known a lot of clergy,' Anne Gawthrop told me, 'and some of them would have made better social workers than priests. Rowan wasn't one of them.' Her husband notes that whenever he arrived half an hour early to serve at an 8 a.m. Eucharist, 'Rowan would always be there praying. I'm very shy. He's the only person who ever gave me the confidence to read out prayers in public.'

Tales of his impact at this time abound. Some friends of Gavin D'Costa, a Catholic theologian at Bristol University, had lost their faith, but returned to the Church after hearing Williams preach in Little St Mary's. Christopher Morgan, best man at his wedding and now religious affairs correspondent of the *Sunday Times*, remembers that 'Rowan did several Holy Weeks at St Luke's, Cardiff, between 1980 and 1990.

Word got round about the quality of his addresses. The congregation grew larger every time.'

The two were introduced by Glyn Simon, Bishop of Llandaff, in 1971. Several years later Morgan became treasurer of the National Union of Students. As one of this body's office-holders, he had been asked to sign a document of welcome for a visiting Soviet delegation, but felt unwilling to do so. He eventually relented under heavy pressure. 'I experienced something of Rowan's qualities at that time,' Morgan says, 'He simply said, "I could never have done that." There was a quiet authority without condemnation. It taught me never to disregard my conscience again.'

Those who think Williams ill-equipped to be Archbishop of Canterbury on the grounds that he has never run a parish may be overlooking the extent of his pastoral experience in his twenties and thirties, let alone more recently. And even some of his colleagues did not know how close he came to returning to Wales for full-time parish work before the post at St George's came up. 'I remember sitting in the Copper Kettle [a town centre café] when he told me this,' says Jane Williams, 'and very much hoping that it wouldn't happen.'

His second book, *Resurrection* (Darton, Longman and Todd, 1982), came out of an invitation from Jim Thompson, Bishop of Stepney, to address clergy in the East End of London on 'interpreting the Easter gospel'. Its conclusion displays the nuanced orthodoxy for which Williams was becoming renowned. We are firstly reminded that the subject has two main features: the tradition in which the apostles hear of the empty tomb discovered by one or more women linked to Jesus; and 'the mature conviction' of Christ's presence in the community gathered for worship: 'an objective word from beyond, a summons and an invitation like the summons and invitation given in the days of his flesh'.[17] The ensuing experiences of conversion and restoration were understood to be produced by Jesus directly, not through the community: 'that there is again a community depends upon an initiative from elsewhere, an initiative more positive than that simply provided by the empty tomb'.[18]

Although Williams finds the empty tomb story 'extremely perplexing', and admits that he 'cannot give any very satisfactory theological and philosophical account of it,' he accepts it none the less as 'a sign of God's historical act' and 'the least difficult interpretation of the New Testament record'.[19] But he repeatedly warns that the empty tomb in itself proves nothing. 'We need to add that no amount of apparitions, however well authenticated, would mean anything apart from the testimony of forgiven lives communicating forgiveness.'[20] The primary evidence for the resurrection is not 'individual report', but the continuing existence of a fellowship marked by restoring grace.

Other aspects of orthodoxy, historical as well as philosophical, absorbed him in this period. He has fond memories of running a graduate seminar on Christology (accounting for the person and work of Christ), and of sessions at the so-called D Society — a fortnightly gathering 'that was an excellent place for mind-sharpening'. A paper not exceeding twenty minutes in length was read out by a don, student or visiting speaker, and followed by an hour and a half of often ferocious debate. Even more than expounding the resurrection, Christology is an inter-disciplinary exercise, and Williams honed his grasp of the subject by keeping up with biblical studies and other areas off his main beat. During the 1980s, as reported, revisionist arguments were being challenged with increasing confidence by theologians keen to show that the creeds were not a betrayal of the biblical evidence from which they purportedly derived. For decades the liberal orthodoxy had been that incarnational ('high') Christology belonged only to the latest strands of the tradition – to the time when the Jesus cult had been plucked from its Jewish roots and transplanted to the foreign soil of Hellenistic culture. This model is now widely thought superficial. Commentators such as Martin Hengel and James Davila have demonstrated that the concept of incarnation was not foreign to the world of first-century Palestinian Judaism, and that some of the most audacious sayings of Jesus (for instance his implied claim to be the embodiment of Torah, God's blueprint for creation, in the Sermon on the Mount) are precisely those that employ Jewish terminology. A measured view of this comes from a scholar such as John Sweet:

> The language and imagery of the New Testament display a Semitic suggestiveness. Its compilers were feeling their way towards the conclusion that Jesus and the Father are one in action. Later theologians, operating in a Hellenistic climate, were more systematic, and used their own language to draw out the metaphysical implications of the scriptural claim.[21]

Williams' summary of Jesus' historical mission quoted earlier in this chapter also owes something to Sweet, who taught him as an undergraduate. But this was only a first step in the argument. That the New Testament does not betray

Jesus' message is a necessary but not sufficient condition for a credible account of incarnational doctrine. In 1982 the editors of the *Theologische Real Encyklopädie* invited Williams to write a substantial article in German on Christological debate during the Middle Ages. The commission was for 20,000 words and involved months of research, mainly among the primary sources. He chiefly learnt that whatever else the incarnation involves, it cannot be about God and man as competing for the same space: it cannot (as he later joked to students) be about explaining how Jesus has an extra bit stuck on, 'giving him a *hypostasis* ['person' or 'substance'] that refreshes the parts others do not reach'. For Williams, the doubters had fallen into a trap through not grasping this point.

The apotheosis of the style he deplored probably came in *The Myth of God Incarnate* (SCM Press, 1977), a collection of essays questioning the divinity of Christ on assorted grounds. Not all seven contributors were from the same stable, but one of their core assumptions emerged in a comment of the editor, John Hick: 'To say, without explanation, that the historical Jesus of Nazareth was also God is as devoid of meaning as to say that this circle drawn with a pencil and paper is also a square.'[22]

Hick's assertion was again questioned by Herbert McCabe. In another withering review, he commented that

> circles and squares and triangles and such occupy their mutually exclusive territories in the common logical world of shapes . . . But just what or where is the common logical world that is occupied in mutual exclusion by God and man? A circle and a square make two

> shapes; a man and a sheep make two animals: God and
> man make two what?[23]

For McCabe and other upholders of orthodoxy, *The Myth of
God Incarnate* was predicated on a defective doctrine of God —
God as a thing whose presence pushes other things out of the
way. In Williams' view, it is only if we see that God and man
do not occupy the same logical space — and thus cannot stand
in a relation of mutual exclusion — that we can understand
what traditional language is meant to convey.

His misgivings about several assumptions behind *The Myth
of God Incarnate* were later brought out in an essay[24] on
another of the contributors, Maurice Wiles (Regius Professor
of Divinity at Oxford, 1970-90), who was known for
drawing unsettling inferences from the cultural remoteness
of the times when the creeds were written. In so far as the
doctrinal claims then made were legitimised in ways that are
now judged indefensible, Wiles held, then they prompt deep
problems for the modern believer.[25] His strategy was to
reframe incarnational doctrine in terms of how Jesus ushered
in new ways of talking about God.

Williams was sensitive to the problem, but unconvinced
by the solution. It was question-begging, he thought, to speak
of Jesus only (or even primarily) in the manner proposed by
Wiles, since 'the language of reconceiving God in the light of
Jesus is irremediably parasitic on a prior apprehension of the
life and death of Jesus as a divine action.'[26] And it was histori-
cally and philosophically naïve to theologise as though 'the
devout imagination could make us coeval with Jesus and the
first believers, so that we can lay hold of the buried pearl of
Jesus' "impact" and yet remain free of those cultural pressures

that lead inexorably towards the errors of doctrine.'[27] Jesus was important for first-century reasons, not for timeless reasons 'distorted by confused first-century minds'. What the New Testament writers actually said was that

> in his ministry and *now*, Jesus is the form which God's judgement takes; that he, then and now, makes real the welcoming mercy of God in the Lord's Supper; that the believer is united with him, that the death and resurrection of Jesus in particular constitute the condition of there being a new humanity.[28]

A wide gap is apparent here. For Wiles, Christ is *illustrative* of 'truths about God which are in principle independent of one particular individual's career', and the doctrinal freight laid on his shoulders by the early Church can be relativised in consequence. For Williams, Christ is *constitutive* for Christian language, 'and for the present reality of the believer's relation to God'.[29]

+━━+

Politics remained a pressing concern. In the early and mid-1980s, the Left talked more about the possible end of civilisation through nuclear war than about the end of Communism. Even at this short historical distance, it can be hard to imagine the ferocity of the ideological clash then being waged. Something of its febrile character is reflected in *The Truce of God* (Fount, 1983), Williams' third book, which combines the case for nuclear disarmament (unilaterally in the first instance as a venture of trust, then multilaterally) with a study of the spiritual sickness said to be reflected in areas such as screen violence and pornography.

At times he grants a point or two to the opposition, for example the multilateralists' complaint of one-sidedness in CND rhetoric.

> They [peace activists] may castigate their own societies and condone the militarism of others. They may reproduce with uncanny accuracy the neuroses of the military establishment, redirected now against government and allies, instead of enemies.[30]

But for the most part his fire is trained on the Right. He sees the arms race and Evil Empire rhetoric as betraying a profound corruption of spirit:

> The flight from dialogue into self-justifying jargon is an aspect . . . of a flight from adulthood, relationship, decision and creativity . . . There is a miserable link between militarised politics, consumer society, the corruption and decline of the arts and the cheapening and trivialising of language – in politics, journalism, advertising and worship . . . This is the vicious circle of the 'developed' world today.[31]

The Truce of God was commissioned as Robert Runcie's Lent Book for 1983, but despite its high spiritual content, there were signs that the then Archbishop was taken aback by all the political salvoes. He probably found the discussion intelligent and provocative and a bit overblown. After all, archbishops of Canterbury operate under all sorts of constraints that do not bind radical young academics.

Williams wasn't slow to follow the dictates of conscience. He and a group of others spent a few hours in the cells on Ash Wednesday, 1985, after they were arrested for scaling the perimeter fence at RAF Alconbury in Cambridgeshire. By then he was Dean of Clare, and his detention provided the college's director of music, Tim Brown, with one of several anxious moments:

> 'Word reached me a few minutes before Evensong was due to start that he would not be able to take the service, but then he never was the most disciplined person in terms of planning. He wouldn't have made a very good precentor.'

His fondness for Williams runs deep none the less. 'The effect he has on people is very uncommon. He's patient and affable, yet you feel you don't want to waste words with him, because his mind is always working overtime.' This comment expresses a view put by others. Brown goes on to observe that 'while everything Rowan says is carefully weighed, he never sounds ponderous. Although he was only with us for two years, it felt much longer. I think that had something to do with his appeal.' Williams also found his Clare years passing happily and too hastily. But as another friend comments, 'you don't turn down the Lady Margaret chair of divinity when it's offered to you.'

◄──►

Until the 1990s, four of the eight professors in the Oxford theology faculty had to be *ex officio* canons of Christ Church Cathedral, and therefore Anglican priests. This has long been resented by scholars from other denominations, though in Williams' case there was agreement that he would also have got the position under a more open recruitment process. Not everything had always landed in his lap — he was shortlisted for the chair of Christian doctrine at King's College London in 1983, for example, but not appointed. Then, a couple of years on, he got a phone call from the outgoing Lady Margaret Professor, John Macquarrie, who said that the post would be his if he wanted it.

Two sides to the next half decade stand out in conversations with Williams' friends. One is that he was 'very good' at the job, in the words of Henry Chadwick, a Cambridge colleague, and added lustre to a faculty that didn't always sparkle. To Oliver O'Donovan, Professor of Moral and Pastoral Theology at Oxford, he was 'a delight', because 'one could always discuss, no holds barred'. Whether on university committees or in cathedral chapter meetings, O'Donovan adds, there was none of the 'carefully judged unclarity'[32] that some detected in Williams' books: 'His ability to grasp where someone was coming from, to enthuse about any positive features he could identify and then to add just a nuance of his own that opened up new possibilities was always evident — one of the gifts that have since made him a superb bishop.'[33] When he preached, colleagues 'made sure not to be away', and the sense of occasion was augmented by 'the sonorous voice, the russified beard, the touch of poetry'. O'Donovan also notes with approval the new Lady Margaret Professor's commitment to Scripture:

> On that point, indeed, Williams will yield nothing to his Evangelical predecessor at Canterbury. 'Why, oh why,' he groaned, when wrestling with yet another ill-judged offering from the Liturgical Commission, 'will they not use the *Bible?*'[34]

The other facet is that for all his success, Williams sometimes felt ill at ease and cut off. Much of the main quadrangle
at Christ Church is filled by six vast clerical homes. A
seventh, where he and Jane moved after their first year, is in
the cathedral cloisters. 'I think living there is like being a
butterfly stuck in a glass case and always exposed to view,'
comments a Catholic contemporary of Williams now teaching nearby. The Oxford faculty building was not a hub or
meeting place like the Cambridge Divinity School. The new
professor made himself accessible by hosting informal open
houses once a week. These were popular events, but could
only go a small way towards reproducing the bonhomie he
had known beforehand. He would no doubt have wanted to
leave academia at some point in any case, given his concern
with taking the gospel to a broader constituency, but the
rarefied conditions in which he lived at Oxford played a part
in the timing.

The electors who gave him his chair wanted him to produce a 'proper' book, as one of them joked, namely a large
work on patristics, his main specialist field. He had begun an
ambitious project on the Arian controversy at Cambridge,
and this was concluded within a few weeks of his installation
at Christ Church. Published as *Arius: Heresy and Tradition*
(Darton, Longman and Todd, 1987; reissued in 2001 by SCM
Press), it involves meticulous scrutiny of the fourth-century
heretic's writings, and fresh speculation about the background that led to his condemnation at the Council of Nicaea
for rejecting the full divinity of Christ. As we have seen,
Williams drew attention to the innovative vocabulary
employed by the orthodox. His subtext was a reminder to
today's conservatives that tradition is organic (the book's

epigraph is Alasdair MacIntyre's remark in *After Virtue* [35] that 'traditions, when vital, embody continuities in conflict'). *Arius* was richly praised, and earned its author a fellowship of the British Academy. Eight months later came the birth of the Williamses' daughter Rhiannon – a particular joy since Jane had suffered several earlier miscarriages.

In the Church at large, the professor assumed a growing public profile in the campaign for women's ordination, especially through his involvement in Affirming Catholicism, the network for liberal Anglo-Catholics established in 1990. He also supported the Lesbian and Gay Christian Movement (LGCM). His perceived liberalism on homosexuality dated from the late 1970s, and involved a familiar strategy. In the first place, he was generous to opponents. He could see that those who deplored all sex outside marriage were often misunderstood. Some forms of liberal polemic dismissed traditionalists as merely ignorant or fearful, but the truest explanation of their stance was that it dovetailed with an even more important matter than sexual ethics: the authority of Scripture. Like the theories of Darwin, pro-gay arguments might knock down more than one theological domino. Williams wanted to reinterpret the relevant texts, and thus to recast the terms of an often sterile debate.

The Bible, he argued, condemns heterosexuals who engage in homosexual acts for gratification, but does not distinguish between gay practice and gay identity. It is therefore unjust to consign to celibacy those who have never known sexual attraction towards the opposite sex, especially since the Old Testament lays so much emphasis on the role of physical love in bonding, not just breeding. Like Robert

Runcie towards the end of his career, Williams thought that the question was resolved one stage back in the argument: faithful gay partnerships could be accepted by all Christians who endorse contraception.

He has qualified this since his appointment to Canterbury, telling his fellow primates in a letter of August 2002 that he will abide by the mind of the Church as reflected in the 1998 Lambeth Conference resolution upholding traditional norms. But his private view remains that an adjustment of teaching on sexuality would not be different from the kind of flexibility now being shown to divorcees who wish to re-marry, or the softening in the sixteenth century of the Church's once total opposition to borrowing with interest, or the nineteenth- and twentieth-century shifts of view on subjects like slavery and eternal hellfire.

The fullest statement of his views came in 'The Body's Grace', a memorial lecture delivered under LGCM auspices[36] in 1989. Drawing partly on the philosopher Thomas Nagel, he defines 'perversion' as 'sexual activity without risk, without the dangerous acknowledgement that my joy depends on someone else's as theirs does on mine'.[37] His conclusion is that 'the worst thing we can do with the notion of sexual fidelity is to "legalise" it in such a way that it stands quite apart from the ventures . . . of growth.'[38] In a Church that accepts birth control, therefore,

> the absolute condemnation of same-sex relations of intimacy must rely either on an abstract fundamentalist deployment of a number of very ambiguous texts, or on a problematic and non-scriptural theory about natural complementarity, applied narrowly and crudely to

physical differentiation without regard to psychological structures. I suspect that a fuller exploration of the sexual metaphors of the Bible will have more to teach us about a theology and ethics of sexual desire than will the flat citation of isolated texts.[39]

More conservative moralists remain divided in their responses to such arguments, but most think that the Bible is clearer than Williams allows, and thus that his interpretation looks wishful. A familiar corollary is regularly drawn from this – that the Anglican Communion might break up unless the old disciplines are restored. The argument has been a source of intermittent dejection to Williams, at least since 1988. In that year a legal move was made by the then Archdeacon of London, George Cassidy, to expel the LGCM from offices they occupied at St Botolph's, Aldgate, on the border between the City and East End. Williams expressed public outrage over this, describing it as 'very scandalous'. But his career was not obstructed by such frankness. Four years later he was approached by representatives of the Church in Wales and invited to become Bishop of Monmouth.

+═══+

This move appears even less surprising in hindsight. He wanted to get out of the theological bunker and had been tipped for high positions in the Church, as well as in academia, for as long as anyone could remember. By this some meant the archbishopric of Wales, and some meant the see of Durham, because of its scholar-bishop tradition. But more meant

Canterbury. A big job would require an apprenticeship, and Monmouth, centred on St Woolos' Cathedral in Newport, had much to be said for it. Williams knew his territory (the diocese's western fringe takes in some of Cardiff's eastern suburbs), and living there brought him closer to his parents. Theories that a shift to another province would handicap him in the Canterbury stakes also look mistaken in perspective. He returned to the Church of England ten years on looking fresher, and with fewer opponents.

But the departure from Oxford provoked anguished reactions all the same. Henry Chadwick, one of his long-standing patrons, looked on Monmouth as a backwater where the new Bishop's talents would be squandered. Even Jane Williams shared this impression at first. 'I felt it was like harnessing a racehorse to a cart,' she told me. 'But I was wrong. Rowan's point was that he knew he could cope with being an academic, but didn't know then about working in a diocese. He wanted another challenge.' A connected point springs from Michael Ramsey's remark about not becoming a theologian till he had been a bishop. Williams wanted 'to learn to listen to a broader range of people'.

The venture succeeded in part because his colleagues let him play to his strengths. Monmouth has about a hundred Anglican parishes. The chief pastor's administrative load is not overwhelming. There is scope for vision, and for taking seriously Williams' own account of the job:

> the extraordinary, taxing and sometimes exhilarating vocation of discerning the signs of resurrection in par-ticular congregations . . . the first task is for the bishop to listen hard . . . for evidence of faith sustained or

rediscovered beyond crisis, of new hopes or projects, new words for evangelism, evidence . . . of old enmities worked through, a drawing towards contemplative delight, of discernment of good and evil in the social environment and of appropriate action within it.

He backed the five church plants (extra-parochial con-gregations and groups) that sprang up around the diocese in his time, and which helped ensure that attendance had risen slightly by the time he moved to Lambeth. Asked to sum up his prescription for outreach and growth, he accepted that non-parochial ventures could have a place alongside the parish system. Pastors should be going to the council estates and other unchurched areas, earning the trust of residents, and 'being on the receiving end of people's hard questions'.[40]

The economic milieu to which he returned was depressed, but due for a more prosperous spell than during the Thatcher years. *The Span of the Cross* (University of Wales Press, 1999), Densil Morgan's history of twentieth-century Welsh Christianity, paints the following picture from close to the turn of the millennium:

> there were numerous signs of rejuvenation and verve. A now diverse economy was slowly growing stronger not only along the M4 corridor in the south but along North Wales' A55 as well. There was now a Welsh film and media industry which . . . was broadly based and international in scope. Cultural life in both languages was dynamic while the Welsh Language Act of 1993 not only safeguarded the rights of both linguistic communi-ties but enhanced substantially the status of Welsh. Welsh-medium education was burgeoning having

secured significant cross-party and government support, while generally there was a feeling of . . . quiet
optimism.[41]

Overall church-going declined throughout the decade,
though, especially in the Nonconformist communities.[42]
Only the Roman Catholics and the newer Evangelical con-
gregations enjoyed something like across-the-board growth.

The Archbishop of Wales, Alwyn Rice-Jones, urged from
the start that a decent amount of time be earmarked for study
in the Bishop of Monmouth's diary. This enabled him to go
away on a speaking engagement one day a week on average,
and to spend about a month a year giving lectures abroad. He
also continued to supervise doctoral students. 'At times this
caused rumblings among the clergy,' says Peter Woodman,
one of Williams' two senior lieutenants until stepping down
as Archdeacon of Monmouth in 2001. 'But most of them
were rather proud of the way that Rowan put the diocese on
the map. It might have been a backwater when he arrived, but
not by the time he left.'

The Archdeacon says he was 'captivated' by the breadth of
Williams' sympathies:

> He was unbelievably kind to me, and to many others. I
> was amazed by how he managed to keep all the balls in
> the air almost all the time. Any vices he had sprang from
> his virtues. He always saw the best in people, and
> several manipulative clerics in the diocese knew how to
> take advantage of him. Sometimes this exasperated
> Keith Tyte [his fellow Archdeacon] and me. We warned
> Rowan about certain characters, and he eventually
> admitted that we had been right. So there was a streak

of holy naïvety in him. I was reminded of Jesus' choice of a man who betrayed him. Rowan also bent over backwards to get on with people who didn't share his outlook, the Evangelicals and Anglo-Catholics who opposed the ordination of women. If there was any loss of morale in the diocese, it was felt by the middle-of-the-road clergy who didn't make a noise or beat a path to his door. They just soldiered on.

The late 1990s saw some of the most melancholy spells in Williams' ministry. Two priests – one of whom apparently took his own life – had been involved in sexual misconduct, and another had to be sacked on the day of his planned induction after an eleventh-hour discovery about his past. These and other considerations – including the possibility that he would be elected Archbishop of Wales – prompted Williams to take on a chaplain, Gregory Cameron. 'Rowan got into the habit of meeting a group of clergy every year to talk about his performance,' Cameron reports.

> In the course of research to give an account of his activities, we established that he was always spending about half of his 80- or 90-hour weeks on the diocese. So he can't be said to have neglected his flock because of all the other activities.
>
> Evangelicals sometimes said they wished he'd preach more from a scriptural text, but basically they liked him. They knew he didn't come from their tradition, and they recognised the efforts he made. But people who think that Rowan is neglectful of others are mistaken. If someone is in need and asks for help, he will strain every sinew for them. On the other hand, he

keeps his own emotional life buttoned up, and is happy to let other people get on undisturbed. Clergy who wanted him to be a nurturing parent were disappointed.

The volume of hate mail sent to the Archbishop grew after the announcement of his appointment to Canterbury. A kind of competition developed between Cameron, Williams and his secretary, Hazel Paling, to open the letters first each morning, and thus to shield the other two from the most venomous. This subject is broached without self-pity in his poem 'First Thing',[43] where Williams, still half-conscious, gets a prelude of the postman's visit from the breaths of his sleeping wife:

> The last bit of the dream is letters falling,
> soft and regular, the papery flutter
> rhythmic on the mat. Not unlike
> grey tides licking sand. Waking
> is water leaking in; the stuff
> out there wobbles and swells
> and settles grudgingly into a dryish
> daytime shape. And the letters
> leaking in resolve themselves
> as the dry short breaths
> of a nextdoor body, finding
> its way out of the night
> into slow breakfast time,
> the food, the light, a few words,
> and the apprehensive, unavoidable
> opening of envelopes.

On Sundays there would be preaching engagements up and down the diocese. Williams also made midweek visits to parishes six to ten times a year, and went into both church and secular schools to give a talk or conduct an assembly several times a month. He set a large store by his contacts with pupils; Woodman judges that he was 'wonderful' in this role. In part, perhaps, to offset suspicion that he didn't get on with nuts and bolts, the Bishop worked assiduously on the Diocesan Board of Finance, and two other bodies, the Parsonage Board and the Diocesan Trust, dealing respectively with fabric and schools. His responsibilities gradually spread further into secular areas. In 2000, for instance, he became President of the Bevan Foundation, a think-tank set up to help co-ordinate community regeneration in Wales.

Some of his best work went on behind closed doors. Word got round that the Bishop was an open-handed counsellor (Gregory Cameron estimates that he saw about a dozen people regularly for much of the 1990s), and much time was also spent in conversation with clerics and candidates for diocesan appointments. No one who worked alongside him thinks that his zeal was muted by family ties – including the unexpected blessing of his son Pip's birth in 1996 – or that his workload led to strains at home. His friends repeatedly highlight his devotion to family; one told me that she knows of 'no one else who has learnt more from their children'.

Of all the forecasts about his time in Monmouth, perhaps the most inaccurate was that a major theological career would be stalled. Williams proved that a mitre was no more an enemy of promise than a pram. Not only did he continue on all cylinders: some people, including his wife, think that the years 1992–2002 saw the best intellectual harvest he had yet enjoyed. Numerous publications appeared, including *Christ on Trial* (Fount, 2000), a study of how each gospel writer presents Jesus' arraignment; *Lost Icons* (T. & T. Clark, 2000), a convoluted but thought-provoking lament over the corruption of values in contemporary society; *Writing in the Dust*, a short reflection on September 11, 2001 (Hodder & Stoughton, 2002); and *Ponder These Things* (Canterbury Press, 2002), an illustrated guide to interpreting icons of Mary. Collaborative projects included *Love's Redeeming Work: The Anglican Quest for Holiness* (Oxford University Press, 2001), a major anthology edited with Geoffrey Rowell and Kenneth Stevenson. Elisabeth Koenig, a professor at the General Theological Seminary in New York, was so impressed by him that she introduced a course on his writings in 1995.

His first two verse collections were *After Silent Centuries* (1994) and *Remembering Jerusalem* (2001); these were reissued with some fresh material as *The Poems of Rowan Williams* (Perpetua Press, 2002). Much of his output falls into discernible clusters. There are poems inspired by places, such as 'Our Lady of Vladimir', 'Pantocrator: Daphni', 'Rublev' and 'Feofan Grek: the Novgorod Frescoes'. Six ('Jerusalem Limestone', 'Gethsemane', 'Calvary', 'The Stone of Anointing', 'Easter Eve: Sepulchre' and 'Low Sunday: Abu Ghosh') sprang from a visit to Jerusalem during Orthodox Holy Week in 1995. Ten more form a section called 'Graves and Gates', and deal with personal loss, including the deaths of his parents and of close friends such as Gillian Rose. *The Poems* ends with translations of works by Rilke, Ann Griffiths (an eighteenth-century farmer's wife), T. Gwynn Jones (a renowned early twentieth-century innovator) and Waldo

Williams (1904–71), 'perhaps the foremost poet of his generation in the Welsh language'.[44]

The Bishop's contributions to the monthly diocesan newsletter give an idea of his range. They typically entail summaries of Christian belief, or attempts to relate an article of the faith to a topical issue. Here is his overview of incarnational teaching, from Easter 1995:

> Jesus, though, is not only tempted as we are, he is, from the first moment of his being, a person in whom the freedom of God is completely at work. In the language of theology, he is completely human and divine. This is not an abstract theory; it means that he understands exactly what we are and what we suffer and why we struggle; but he is never overwhelmed because there is no obstacle in him to the action of God at every moment. What he's doing is what God's doing.

He shows diplomatic instincts over the Middle East crisis in May 2000, arguing that 'the long and dreadful history of Jews living among Christians as perpetual victims has created in modern Israel a culture of insecurity transformed into the aggressive determination never to be a victim again.' He gives short shrift to Protestant fundamentalists and Orthodox Jews who claim a scriptural warrant for their view that Israel is entitled to the fullest extent of Solomon's kingdom, retorting that the passage concerned (in Leviticus 25) has God tell the Israelites that no one possesses any piece of the Land necessarily and for ever, and that it is given to Israel to be administered for the common good:

> The fanatical grabbing of land for new settlement and

(for example) the policies of modern Israel about access to fresh water for the non-Jewish people are very much at odds with Jewish Scripture – and this is recognised by many Jews in Israel.

At Christmas 2001, he moves on to the sensitive question of Christian–Muslim dialogue. Mentioning the theory that Muhammad was deterred from possible conversion to Christianity by the scale of internal church conflicts, Williams stresses what is admirable in Islam before explaining why his allegiances lie elsewhere:

> Islam has a wonderful vision of divine majesty, generosity and glory, and its demand for unreserved loving obedience has great nobility. But it is a faith that cannot find room either for the idea that God longs to share his very life or for the vision of a God who can only win through defeat. It is not intrinsically a violent faith, but it is one that sets high store by victory. And it is not able to pray to God in God's own 'voice', to say 'Father' in the Spirit of Jesus.

He praises the Alpha Course as 'the single most popular and straightforward introduction to the Christian faith on the market at present'. Acknowledging the familiar complaints (that it can seem manipulative, narrow in its doctrine, and appears oriented towards the middle classes), he also underlines some of the positives: 'Yes, the impression is of a middle-class core . . . Then you realise that, in fact, several of these new church plants are in deeply deprived areas and that they clearly do relate to local people and draw them into leadership.'

A missive just before the 2001 General Election commends four criteria for Christians preparing to vote that are a long way from the top of any mainstream party's priorities. First, the relief of Third World debt. (He makes the questionable claim that 'the greater part of the world's population lives in a downward spiral of poverty', but is clearly right in adding that Third World deprivation is 'hugely intensified by debt to wealthier nations or banking institutions'.) Next, he expresses alarm over a House of Commons vote to allow the cultivation of human embryos for the cloning of genetic material:

> We already permit the creation of 'spare' embryos for fertility research and treatment. We are now, it seems, reconciled to the creation of potentially independent human organisms for research, which can be discarded when they have served their turn. Has our liberal abortion law made us insensitive to the basic principle that no human individual is there simply for the 'use' of another?'

Thirdly, he supports the idea of 'a programme for regenerating our agriculture through organic methods' as a response to the foot-and-mouth crisis. His last consideration repeats one of his main arguments in *Lost Icons*, that

> real spiritual education in schools happens when children are in an atmosphere where all kinds of things (not just the odd lesson on personal development or religious studies) puts them in touch with a vital, coherent picture of how a good life is lived. This gets more remote the more teachers are weighed down with admin and testing – and the more they themselves lack a coherent picture of how life is well lived.

The Williams style travelled well. An address to church people in or out of the diocese could be relied on to put an apparently unpromising subject in a fresh light. Examples include his talks on giving to the 1996 Stewardship Advisers' National Conference, which came at the subject from a trinitarian angle. To receive something from God is not (despite the crude models that have arisen in both the Catholic and Protestant traditions) to have a possession, Williams insists.

> It is to be caught up in the stream of God's action . . . And if we begin from . . . the life of God as Trinity, the gift of God as the gift of God's own life, we shall come by a roundabout route to what I always think is one of the basic principles of sensible thinking about stewardship: that it is given to us to become givers.

His longer pieces include a talk on the untenability of secularism (discussed in the next chapter), and a detailed response to Pope John Paul's request for ecumenical advice on reforming the papacy. Williams combines a call for change with an apologia for Anglicanism. Scripture is inconclusive about a Petrine office, he argues, but 'suggestive as regards a Petrine charism – the gift of pointing to the Church's one foundation in the power of God manifest in Jesus' resurrection'. Tradition accepts a carrying forward of a Petrine charism in the church of Peter and Paul, represented by its bishop, but is unclear in the early centuries what this means:

> Rome is a touchstone of right belief, but not automatically a settler of disputes or an indispensable element in determining the limits of Catholic communion. Later claims by and for the Roman see are destructive of the

whole ecological balance of order and sacrament and doctrine in the Church.

Williams concludes that the hazier style of leadership embodied by the Archbishop of Canterbury reflects strength in weakness:

> It might be said that the fragility and potential fragmentation of Anglicanism internationally only shows the importance of giving proper executive authority to a chief pastor. But I'd rather argue that the difficulties of this office simply show the real state of international Christianity: it *is* culturally varied, and centralising authority increasingly doesn't work, except by doing some violence to local church life (and often not even then). The Anglican situation, about which I have no illusions of grandeur or success, means that the Communion's focus has no option but to acknowledge the weakness of the unifying gospel in the face of cultural and political diversity, and to let the hope of the gospel speak from, not against, that acknowledged weakness.

As I have said, a full record of Williams' achievements cannot be given in these pages. That will be a task for his biographers in due time. But even on this small canvas, four events that shaped his life before his move to Lambeth need mentioning: the decision in 1996 to allow women priests in Wales, the Lambeth Conference two years later, his election as Archbishop of Wales in 2000, and his brush with death on September 11, 2001.

The vote on women at the Church in Wales' Governing

Body followed the same decision in England four years earlier. As elsewhere, the joy of the majority was attended by dismay among opponents. Between 10 and 15 per cent of parishes in Williams' diocese affiliated themselves to Credo Cymru – the umbrella group for traditionalists, corresponding to England's Forward in Faith – but only a third of these opted for the minstrations of the so-called Provincial Assistant Bishop, who in any case provides 'additional' (not, as in England, 'alternative') oversight. Although he was seen as a prime advocate of the change, conservatives ended up feeling grateful to Williams, as several made clear in letters to the *Church Times*.

He found aspects of the Lambeth Conference intensely depressing. The only aspect of it that drew real media interest was a resolution reaffirming the traditional line on homosexuality. This accentuated the common assumption that the Church is obsessed with monitoring what goes on behind the bedroom door. The 800 or so delegates were divided into four groups with separate agendas relating to mission, ministry, education and morality. From these smaller formations they emerged to debate several subjects, including sexuality, in plenary sessions; and at that stage all but about 60 voted for an essentially hard-line motion prohibiting all sex outside marriage. The liberal plea for a casting aside of fear and prejudice over the issue was furiously denounced by many African and Asian bishops as a capitulation to 'decadent' Western values. There were few signs of the emphasis on negotiation and 'taking time' that Williams (who abstained in the vote) holds dear.

Mark Santer, then Bishop of Birmingham, recalls the process as 'wholly unacceptable'. Since the issue 'had only been discussed in detail by a quarter of the delegates, and it had taken them a full fortnight to really start listening to each other', he says, it was

> absurd to think that a snap decision could be reached by a full gathering of the bishops in one hot afternoon. After all, it took the various groups at the Second Vatican Council several years to resolve their differences. The motion's patchwork quality was underlined by a clause speaking of the need to listen to lesbian and gay Anglicans. This looked self-contradictory.

For Santer and other dissenters, the heart of the problem was that 'African bishops, with some justice, given the history of misconduct by missionaries, tend to associate homosexuality with paedophilia. They do not reckon with faithful relationships between adults.' Both sides felt beleaguered, however. Some observers saw in the vehemence of various Third World delegates a justified response to a secularising agenda in wealthy countries like the United States.

Williams was saved from Evangelical wrath at the time by his being chairman of the sub-group discussing mission. 'Making Moral Decisions', the title of his address to one of the conference's plenary gathering, had a more abstact flavour – though its message was only lightly coded. His principal argument was that Christian identity has more to do with certain patterns of life than with adherence to the rule book:

> What we are looking for in each other is the grammar of obedience: we watch to see if our partners take the same kind of time, sense that they are under the same

kind of judgement or scrutiny . . . This will not guarantee agreement; but it might explain why we should always first be hesitant and attentive to each other . . . If another Christian comes to a different conclusion and decides in different ways from myself, and if I can still recognise their discipline and practice as sufficiently like mine to sustain a conversation, this leaves my own decisions to some extent under question.[45]

He illustrated the point with his own belief that no Christian should ever support the possession of weapons of mass destruction, and then conceded that many others took a different view – 'not thoughtless, shallow, uninstructed Christians, but precisely those who make themselves accountable to the central truths of our faith'.

+━━◆━━+

The Bishop suffered a double bereavement in 1999: his father and mother died within a short time of each other. He wrote an 'intensely personal' poem for each of them. 'Ceibr: Cliffs',[46] for Aneurin Williams, makes use of nature to encompass the loss:

> The quilt of willowherb muffles
> the stream before it drops
> invisible to the beach;
> the moist whisper thinned
> in its straight seaward fall,
> the shore sound coming back up, dry
> as two palms rubbing steadily
> close to your ear, or pages

fingered through, or a hand
stroking an unshaved cheek, hard;
or a thick old fabric, tearing
very slowly...

Preferment seemed likely at this time. Rice-Jones retired in July, and many considered Williams to be the natural successor. He was elected five months later. In supporting him, Barry Morgan, Bishop of Bangor, said that several others would make worthy archbishops, but Williams would be a great one. Wales has no first see. The primate remains in charge of his diocese, whichever it is. Williams' additional duties entailed a higher profile in the media, on ecumenical platforms, and in the committees and debates of the Church's Governing Body. He continued to travel frequently outside the province, and it was as a roving teacher that he witnessed the assault on the Twin Towers. When it happened he was addressing about twenty-five people in an office next to Trinity Church, Wall Street, two blocks from the World Trade Center. The group didn't emerge from the building for several hours, having been advised against moving. Half-choked by dust, they were among the wraith-like figures escorted away by the fire brigade to a waiting ferry. Commenting on the catastrophe for the *Church Times* twenty-four hours later, he spoke of his mounting sense of what life in Jerusalem or Baghdad was like all the time. 'I'm obviously very glad to be alive, but also feel deeply uncomfortable, and my mind shies away from the slaughter.'

Within a few weeks Williams had completed *Writing in the Dust*, which was published soon after as a small paperback. He remarked on the contrast between the religious murderers who made 'a martyr's drama out of a crime', and the non-religious witness through desperate mobile phone calls 'to what religious language is supposed to be about' – the triumph of gratuitous love. For the victims, he thought, 'the hardest thing in the world is to know how to act so as to make the difference that *can* be made; to know how and why that differs from the act that only releases or expresses the basic impotence of resentment.'[47] These were counted wise words, even though some felt that his efforts to understand the terrorists made him an insufficiently harsh judge of their crimes. Such critics detected ambiguity in his saying both that the fanatics had a choice,[48] and that they experienced 'their world as leaving them no other option'.[49] His defenders argued that he was simply anatomising the deluded mindset.

A year later, his main ground for opposing war with Iraq was the fear that removing an unjust regime 'without reference to international law' would be opening a Pandora's box, and that coalition action would invite a spiral of terrorist retaliation:

> This does not depend on the sponsorship of any one state. There may also be a consolidation of anti-Western feeling and a worsening of the situation in Israel. If Arab neighbours are convinced they are excluded from the process of containment of Saddam, the results will be disastrous. If they are willing to sign up to diplomatic containment and indictment in international courts, we should work with this.[50]

These words express a long-held view, also reflected in his denunciation of the Afghanistan conflict in late 2001. Whatever the merits of his stand, it was felt by many to augur badly for his chances of further promotion. The issue surged in importance in January 2002, when George Carey announced that he would be bowing out nine months later. Named as one of three frontrunners, with Bishops Richard Chartres of London and Michael Nazir-Ali of Rochester, Williams was held to be further handicapped by his supposed enthusiasm for disestablishment, as well as by his admission to having ordained a gay man with a partner. Some commentators believe that Carey, too, was against him, and that Williams' chances of translation to Southwark four years previously had been frustrated after he declined to give the then Archbishop an assurance that he would toe the agreed line on sexual morality.

He rejects this as an 'urban myth', insisting that 1998 would have been the wrong time for a move back to England, and that his relations with Carey were always good. As with Southwark, the tale of his eventual emergence as top choice for Canterbury has been heavily laced with conjecture about manoeuvrings among the fifteen clerical and lay selectors who make up the Crown Appointments Commission. One theory has it that his place as the commission's top choice was leaked, in order to stop the Prime Minister from choosing the second candidate on the list of two names with which Downing Street is always presented. Other sources say that Tony Blair was enthusiastic about the Archbishop of Wales all along.

For his supporters, what counts is that the selection reflected the triumph of imagination over faint-heartedness. He was repeatedly endorsed by influential church figures and others, many of whom felt that his suitability was boosted by a perceived lack of intellectual leadership in the Church

Aneurin and Delphine Williams on their wedding day,
Ystradgynlais parish church, 1948.

Growing up:
Above: Rowan Williams with his
mother in 1950, and (*left*) as a
youngster in 1953 and (*right*) in
1955 . . .

... (*left*) on his first visit to London in 1959; (*below*) as a choirboy at All Saints', Oystermouth in 1963 and (*below left*) as a young man in 1968.

Graduation at Christ's College, Cambridge, 1971.

With Jane Paul, on their wedding day, 1981.

Consecration as Bishop of Monmouth, 1992.

With some of his fellow-delegates at the Lambeth Conference of 1998.

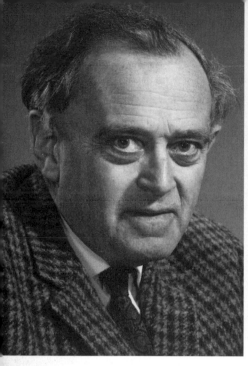

Above left: Donald MacKinnon
Above right: Gillian Rose
Below left: Vladimir Lossky
Below right: Ludwig Wittgenstein

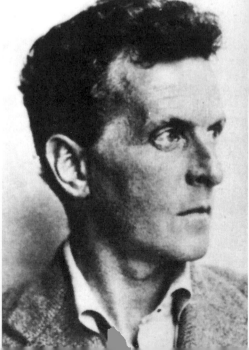

Relaxing after a Monmouth diocesan pilgrimage to Walsingham, 1997.

Overleaf: The enthronement as Archbishop of Canterbury,
Canterbury Cathedral, 2003.

during the 1990s. Asked in November 2002 to identify himself with one of two familiar camps – those who complain of
too much structure in the Church, and those who complain
of too much liberty – the Archbishop of Canterbury-elect
spoke of an alternative picture based on gratitude. He regret-
ted that this quality ('the sense that something has been
given, which we're struggling to articulate and respond to')
was not considered fundamental.

> Liberty focuses on what suits me, and makes me feel all
> right, but doesn't have this overwhelming feeling of
> what's been given. Structure that tells you exactly
> what's been given and exactly what you must do with it
> has the same effect.[51]

If the whole of the Church of England were gathered to
hear his rallying cry for the years ahead, it would be

> that you are here because God wants you to be here.
> And God's wanting you to be here has been mediated to
> you by centuries of mixed but exciting and imaginative
> witness within this tradition. Be thankful for that wit-
> ness, and how it has made the reality of God's welcome
> complete for you. And, in the life you lead, attempt to
> point back into that history, not for the sake of a dead
> tradition but for what it livingly conveys of God's wel-
> come and God's call. Try not to look so obsessionally at
> each other all the time, to see how we're doing. There's
> a good deal in spiritual tradition that suggests the worst
> thing you can do is to look at each other with rivalry
> rather than with gratitude or shared delight.[52]

The message is as unsettling to the Evangelical groups who

want Williams to resign as it is welcome to many in the
Anglican mainstream. This is not the place for a round-up of
secular opinion, still less for forecasts about whether
Williams can make an impact on the vast majority of people
in Britain who have little or no connection with the Church.
But one representative view merits a mention in passing. It is
summed up by A. N. Wilson, a sometimes vinegary observer,
who became a novelist after losing his faith at theological
college. Like many others, he got acquainted with Williams
through his poems. Wilson notes that they are often set on
holy ground. 'Yet the preoccupations are those of an earthy
mystic who loves women ...' That Williams has ended up in
Lambeth Palace rather than in some faraway university can be
counted an extraordinary blessing, Wilson suggests. He goes
on to quote the last two stanzas of 'Cornish Waters', a verse
meditation on water that was inspired by the town of
Camelford, and written 'in honour of regional water
companies'[53]:

> Rain sours in the ruts of foresight, payment
> salts it to piss, so that it cannot fall
> cold on a breaking skin, graceful
> for tongue and stomach.
>
> Rain's not exhausted, can't be wooed to go;
> the dark still gathers out of which,
> heavy and wet as words or grace, it falls
> to wash sores; flood banks.

Reading this poet now, concludes Wilson, 'is like feeling the
first drops of rain after a long season of drought'.[54]

Chapter Two

+>==<+

PHILOSOPHY AND THEOLOGY

Beyond the Secular

W HERE IS PHILOSOPHICAL TRUTH to be sought – in a set of correct propositions abstracted from any particular context, or in the cultivation of what Andrew Shanks terms 'conversational skill'? Ludwig Wittgenstein (1889–1951) started by giving the first answer, and then abandoned it for the second. He did so in pre-theological terms. He began as an extreme positivist, aiming at a doctrine so far as possible independent of linguistic tradition, at the furthest possible remove from poetry, therefore; as close as possible to mathematics, completely excluding theology. But he rejected that ambition in his later work. And for Shanks,

> this turn then points back towards the possibility of theology. Because wisdom comes from skill in conversation ... [And] what counts, for theology, is 'conversational' skill in the rich appropriation of church tradition. This is what Rowan Williams believes in very deeply.

But Wittgenstein is more accurately described as an agnostic than a believer – though he applied unsuccessfully to join the Benedictine Order, and on his deathbed agreed to let a friend read the work of theologians including Barth to him. Williams still reveres Wittgenstein, but at least since the early 1990s his thought has evinced the strong influences of Gillian Rose, and, through her, Hegel's bid to distil the insights of religion in conceptual form.

Rose, sometime Professor of Social and Political Thought at Warwick University, was baptised into the Church of England several hours before she died in 1995, at the age of forty-eight. She had met the then Lady Margaret Professor at a conference some years before, and they struck up a rapport which he describes as hugely important to him. Rose was drawn to Christianity through pondering the implications of her moral and political convictions. Though very different from Wittgenstein, she has in common with him a concern about conversational skill, not the pursuit of abstract propositional correctness. For her, Shanks suggests, 'everything depends on the cultivation of a maximum intellectual restlessness which comes to rest neither in any dogma, nor in any sort of settled scepticism.' The process of her conversion took its initial impetus from her understanding of our condition as thinking agents in the world. In Rose's picture, a thought involves a commitment, and is therefore a kind of 'staking' or 'violence', because beliefs entail opposition to other beliefs. But no negation can be final, since this would be the end of thinking as such. One set of assertions is followed by another set of assertions, and out of both sets a resolution may follow. Self-examined mental life reflects this course: it involves a move away from solipsism and self-preoccupation. Rose moralises the process, arguing that it works as love does. 'What brought her to baptism is the belief that thinking and loving are connected,' Williams explains. And it is this insight, for Rose and other Hegelian Christians, that places us on a path leading from logic to theology, with credible tools for justifying an apparently daring extrapolation.[1]

Hegel (1770–1830) endorsed elements of the traditional 'proofs' for the existence of God, termed 'the Absolute', through projecting the conditions of thought to their most refined degree possible. As Williams argues, 'to think about thinking is to think about, or rather *within*, an infinite relatedness, a comprehensive intelligibility.'[2] The Absolute can be defined as the ungrounded or self-grounded reality without which there is nothing thinkable; and for the Hegelian Christian, this reality must have some connection with what can be thought. If the link between thinking and loving is granted, then a similar association may be conceived between the Absolute and loving as well.

Williams has defended Hegel's compatibility with trinitarian orthodoxy, among other claims, in his scholarly writings.[3] Here we need only note his debt to the Hegelian scheme, and especially its portrayal of the incarnation, crucifixion, resurrection and outpouring of the Holy Spirit as grids on which to understand the processes of loss and return that characterise thought, and history itself. This perspective is corroborated by Andrew Shanks, who describes Hegelian philosophy as 'profoundly trinitarian and christological; interpreting the central dogmas of Christian faith precisely as a symbolic celebration of the very deepest philosophic thoughtfulness'.

So a theologian renowned for wariness about intellectual systems has drunk deeply from the well of one of philosophy's supreme systematicians. This would be a greater paradox but for the centrality of self-displacement and negotiation in Hegel's thought. 'Hegel is for ever trying to open conversation up, not close it down,' says Shanks. 'This is also very much Rowan's style.' How might Hegelian perspectives be applied in the public realm? A hint of what the Archbishop has in mind comes in his Raymond Williams lecture,[4] delivered at the 2002 Hay-on-Wye literary festival. Characteristically, his conclusion that hard-line secularism motors on a punctured tyre is balanced by a critique of corrupt forms of religion.

Though acknowledging a difficulty about definitions (Hegel favoured certain forms of secularism, albeit in his own very different setting), Williams begins by suggesting that a secularist set of protocols for life today would rest on 'the assumption that our attitudes have to be determined by factors that do not include any reference to agencies or presences beyond the tangible'. Some groups will have beliefs and commitments that thereby become inadmissible in wider discourse, and if these beliefs are to find public expression, they must be recast in ways that are acceptable to those who don't share them. One consequence of this is that religious believers (among others) will have to dress in borrowed clothes; another is that the 'definitive currency' of the public realm will be seen as being to do with calculations about functions. Williams then surmises that 'secularism in its neat distillation is inseparable from functionalism'. It will generate policies and practices dominated by 'instrumental or managerial considerations', since other kinds of perspective will be confined to the private sphere.

The argument then turns to a definition of the 'unsecular' perspective. Initially Williams traces it in the life of the imagination and in art, quoting from T. S. Eliot's 'Burnt Norton': 'the unseen eyebeam crossed, for the roses / Had the look of flowers that are looked at.' For Williams, it is the imaginative awareness evoked by these lines that secularism undermines, since the non-secular fundamentally involves a readiness to see 'things or persons as the objects of another sensibility than my own; perhaps also another sensibility than our own, whoever "we" are, even if the "we" is humanity itself'. In other words, non-secular people view the object of their apprehensions as being in important respects not defined by their own awareness.

The point can be sharpened if we include our own subjectivity as one of those objects of awareness that elude our possession. And good art 'works to make present an aesthetic object that allows itself to be contemplated from perspectives . . . other than those of the artist's own subjectivity.' By contrast, hard-line secularism

> fails by bidding for an ultimately exclusive, even antihumanist closure; it looks to a situation in which we are not able to see the world and each other as always and already seen, in the sense that we acknowledge our particular perspective to be shadowed by others that are inaccessible to us.

This, for Williams, is why secularism can be considered a mirror image of fundamentalism, especially in its Muslim and Christian forms. In Williams' picture, secularism exists because of the ease with which religion can confuse 'faith or knowledge directed towards God and the knowledge exercised by God', and thereby become a system of control and violence. He can thus argue not just that secularism and religious fundamentalism feed off each other, but, more subtly, that fundamentalism represents a secularising moment within religion. He is perhaps too coy in acknowledging just how many Christians, let alone non-believers, see discipleship in just the blunt terms that he deplores. But his view has undeniable underpinnings in the tradition.

The second half of the lecture involves further ruminations on the apparently paradoxical need to make religion 'unsecular', and some suggestions about how this can be done through further thought about art. Aware of the glibness in seeing art as a religious enterprise, Williams is keen to emphasise the connections nevertheless. 'Do the roses look as if they were flowers that were loved?' he asks, and, if so, what would that mean?

The process described is complex. As a viewer, I recognise that what lies before me, 'whether rose or person', can be seen from other perspectives than mine. I acknowledge 'the inaccessibility that this entails and the necessary relation of time and understanding in such a light', and am then driven to ask what a 'maximally comprehensive' seeing or reading of the person or object might be. The answer is, one that had unrestricted time to look. But having unrestricted time to look assumes 'a constancy or commitment to looking, thus a self-investment, even self-dispossession, in respect of what is seen or read'. And if we put the taking of time 'at the centre of truthful understanding', then a convergence of understanding and love comes into sharper focus:

The aesthetic sense of inaccessibility is on the edge of

particular kinds of moral evaluation, seeing in the light of someone's (actual or possible) love; it is not the same thing, but it would be hard to make full sense of the one without the other. And the moral in turn borders on the religious, in the sense that the religious believer is committed to affirming the moralist's possible love as actual. There is a perspective that we can only speak of as representing unrestricted time, total self-investment: for the Buddhist, say, that is the perspective of the objectless compassion of enlightenment; for the Christian (or Jew or Muslim), it is the perspective of an active creator . . .

So self-displacement or self-questioning forms a central element in the kind of religion that Williams is commending – not from a sense that we can't be sure about things, and had better reserve judgement, but out of fidelity to orthodoxy.

He warns that this is not to argue for a theocratic model of government, however benign. His plea is that secularism should at least be prepared 'to secure the participation of religious communities in public business', especially in education, and to be willing to discuss policy in broader terms than those of 'instrumental reason'. Coleridge, quoted with approval by Williams, conceived of the religious establishment's relationship to the secular power as one of friendly opposition, with the Church acting as 'the compensating counterforce': whatever is 'beneficent and humanising in the aims, tendencies, and proper objects of the State, the Christian Church collects in itself as in a focus, to radiate them back in a higher quality.'[5]

Among other things, this argument ought to help recast the

sometimes tired terms of debate over issues such as church schools. What Williams calls 'procedural secularism' protests at a violence of the imagination in religion 'that seeks to control all meanings in virtue of its comprehensiveness and intensity'. But such secularism must itself be challenged by the efforts of 'imagination' in order to 'resource and renew motivation within our common life'. And understood in this way (in Coleridge's sense as well as Williams'), imagination must also leave some space for authentic religion.

The lecture was criticised by Christians, as well as atheists. Richard Cross, an Oxford philosopher and former student of Williams, was struck by 'how *a priori* and unhistorical' it looked: 'It seems astonishing to hold that (only?) a non-secular way of life can allow one to understand that there are different viewpoints, and thus allow a genuine dialogue. I'd have thought that as a matter of history, the art of negotiation and compromise seems far more a mark of secular life than of religious.' Others found themselves pulled in both directions. 'Cross' complaint qualifies the Archbishop's argument without invalidating it,' said another. 'The thesis appears more plausible when expressed with due tentativeness.'

Some of Williams' other interventions have also been considered more persuasive when interpreted in a milder form. An example from 2002 was his Dimbleby Lecture, with its worries about the rise of the so-called market state. Those who thought he was decrying most of the economic changes in Britain of the past two decades accused him of talking nonsense.[6] Those who interpreted him as saying something more modest – namely that there is 'a space where public morality, local loyalty and a sense of community used to be', in one columnist's words[7] – were much more complimentary.

The Incarnation

Whether and how far theology should ally itself with other disciplines is a conundrum nearly as old as the Church. Williams takes an intermediate view. As we have seen, he is happy to take inspiration from philosophers and others who can open up paths to religious commitment. No less than in the patristic period, today's theologians can strive to produce ever more effective accounts of Christian belief in conversation with the broader culture. But he also thinks that care is needed: theology should avoid endorsing any one kind of contemporary reasoning or intellectual system. As an upholder of orthodoxy, Williams also wants to warn that personal intuitions

> only become part of a really transforming process when seen in the light of something more far-reaching. In the New Testament, 'faith' is the name of that condition of life created through the death and resurrection of Jesus; it is the rebirth that lies on the far side of an entry into, a 'yielding' to, this mystery.[8]

This forms a further reason for Williams' belief in the inseparability of theology and spirituality. Picking up on a remark of John of the Cross, he says that 'theologians like myself know that their failures of understanding are actually failures of praying.'[9]

How is this to be understood in relation to the person and work of Christ? To start with, says Williams, there is the 'distinctive' character of Christian prayer. The prayer that Christians offer out of faith in God as Trinity is not a petition addressed from one agent to another, a movement from here to there. 'Christian prayer is an entry to a life that is not ours, a life so rich, so abundant, that we can't actually grasp it, that lives *us*.' This is indeed what many Christians report: that prayer involves contact 'with one who is both other and not other'. The experience is one of communion but not absorption, and this means that in Williams' view, it is wrong to see prayer as being about creating a relationship with God. Rather, prayer involves 'a dropping into what is there'.

He ties this argument to the historical record, arguing that such new ways of praying came about through Jesus' earthly life. Building on the summaries already quoted, he notes the well-attested claim that Christ spoke with authority. For Williams, he 'seems to be saying: "How you relate to what I am and what I say is going to shape how you relate to God."' God is seeking to re-create a people for himself, but his people have fallen apart. The Law, notionally a fount of divine grace, has become a means of disowning those who can't comply with all its provisions. God, however, declares that any who welcome his word are acceptable:

> And when Jesus invites somebody for a drink at his house, that is functionally equivalent to God telling people that they're accepted . . . that's quite a bold thing for anybody to say, and that is one of those obstinate things in the gospel tradition that won't go away, however much of the acid of criticism you drip upon it.

By what he says and does, then, Jesus claims to be rewriting the rule book and redefining what it means to belong to God's people:

He is acting like the God who chose Israel in the first place. In the Old Testament God had chosen his cluster of slaves to be a people; and Jesus, in choosing his fishermen, tax collectors and prostitutes, repeats and re-embodies this moment of choice: he claims a creative liberty for himself that belongs strictly to God.

But the other very arresting quality displayed by Jesus is that his gaze is always directed away from himself towards the God of Israel 'with whom he, it seems, senses an intimacy that can only be expressed in very drastic, very revolutionary terms'. This was perhaps the hardest question faced by the early Church: how to designate a man who appeared utterly dependent and utterly free – who claimed a divine liberty and who was yet so obedient to God that you couldn't accuse him of trying to stand in the Father's place.

And as we have also noted, the effect of Jesus' career was so extraordinary that it took centuries for the Church to reconceive its doctrine of God. Gradually there arose a conviction that God is not only source, but also loving response; that there is in God 'the agency of giving that we call Father; in God there is also a derivative responding agency that we call the Son or the Word, and that these powers, agencies, whatever you want to call them, are equal.'

Belief that Christ was 'of one substance with the Father' did not become normative until the fourth century. The length of time taken to arrive at this definition was caused by a sense of the unsatisfactoriness of apparently neater theories. Some patristic theologians were happy to think of God in purely transcendent and monistic terms, and then to speak of Jesus as a deputy: the view that 'God can't do everything,' as

Williams comments, 'and the slightly messy and time-consuming business of running the universe and saving the human race might appropriately be delegated to a sort of divinity who wasn't quite on the same level.'

He sees this model as doubly defective: it won't do justice to the absolute creative freedom felt to have been at work in Jesus, or to the 'exhilarating possibilities' that Christians believed had been opened up for them by the crucifixion and resurrection. On what Williams calls the 'unadventurous' model of God and his deputy, what was promised was an authorised communication from God that would help us to lead better lives and to pray with a bit more confidence. But a bolder claim was made by other Christians – that our goal is communion with God, not merely communication with him. Thus, Williams argues, developed orthodoxy expresses 'the belief that in God, to put it very simply, there is room for us. Because in God there is not only that eternal giving, there is an eternal answering. And we can echo and take in and embody that answer, that loving response.'

The doctrine of the incarnation states that there is a full human identity in Christ, which is 'at every moment of its being suffused . . . with the life of the divine answer to the [originating] divine love.' Precisely how this happened is a mystery on which the Church must remain reticent, even though new insights into the belief may arise from time to time. 'Getting all that straight is a nightmare job, and nobody has really done it,' Williams admits. 'I can't say how; I can say what.' And the 'what' in this instance 'is a human life that erects no obstacles to the activity of God at any time.' In 1998 he produced a précis of his argument in a rebuke to Jack Spong, an American bishop, whose public rejection of historic Christianity was based on a caricature. Incarnational teaching, Williams wrote,

> does not claim that the 'theistic' God (i.e. a divine individual living outside the universe) turns himself into a member of the human race but that this human identity, Jesus of Nazareth, is at every moment, from conception onwards, related in such a way to God the Word (God's eternal self-bestowing and self-reflecting) that his life is unreservedly and uniquely a medium for the unconstrained love that made all things to be at work in the world to remake all things.[10]

To return to the start of Williams' argument, all the theological speculation springs from the Christian experience of prayer and of lives transformed. And because the life of God includes an element of depending and responding, there is room in God for us:

> We can become, very much in inverted commas, 'divine'; that is to say, we can embody some aspects of the divine love, without denying our dependence and our limitedness as creatures . . . So we don't have, in order to be united with the life of God, to deny that we are mortal. We don't have to deny that we are vulnerable. And here is surely good news in a very dramatic form.

The Church also holds that an axe was laid to the roots of evil through the passion and resurrection. There is no doctrine of the atonement purporting to explain how this came about, only a variety of theories, some of which reflect Christian divisions. Williams' account accords with most shades of mainstream opinion. First, the nature of the cross: it is less about the extremity of suffering than about the extremity of helplessness. 'To walk with Jesus and the God of Jesus . . . is to risk becoming a cypher in someone else's scheme of things.'[11] The cross, therefore, is 'a gateway into that strange community in which non-citizens belong together because they belong to God'.[12]

What makes the crucifixion of Jesus different from that of other victims is that it is done to someone who claims to speak for God: 'He promises being with God and his path leads to the cross; so that we are starkly challenged as to whether we can cope with identifying this place of execution as God's place.' That is why it makes sense to speak of the cross as an action as well as a passion, for 'it is the sign and the substance of God's decision to be where his human creation tries hardest to kill itself.' And for Williams, the 'price' paid through the crucifixion is not to do with placating God's wrath, but with the way in which 'the bearer of God's life bears the consequence of human self-hatred, the cost of human fear.'[13]

The Holy Spirit

So incarnational doctrine arises through a mixture of historical analysis and a pondering on the 'logic' of Christian prayer. Williams' discussion of the Holy Spirit's divinity takes a similar form. In this case he responds to the common attitude that has no problem in accepting divine duality – the Father as God transcendent and the Son as God immanent, for example – but shies away from full-bloodied trinitarianism. In doing so he displays greater metaphysical confidence

than is thought warrantable by many contemporary theologians. As a traditionalist influenced by Eastern Orthodoxy,
he believes that trinitarian language tells us something about
the divine nature, not merely (as often in Western theology)
about three ways in which God is felt to be at work.

'Spirit', a term used only rarely in the Old Testament, is a
way of talking about the presence and power of God, notably
in Exodus 36, where it is represented as inspiring an artist in
his work. In the New Testament, the Spirit is often referred
to in connection with Jesus: God, says Paul, sends the Spirit
of his Son into our hearts (e.g. Romans 8:26 ff.). John's
Gospel portrays the Spirit of truth coming from the Father,
and showing us the truth about Jesus: 'It's as if all that enormous force, the cosmic wind, the shaping energy in Hebrew
Scripture, has all gathered itself into a point in the life of
Jesus.' And in consequence, God's presence in the world as
Spirit works to create the likeness of Christ. The Holy Spirit
enables Christians 'to pray in Jesus' way', and despite a tendency throughout church history to cut off the Spirit and see
it as just a sign or agent of divine power, Williams insists that
from very early on the Spirit was seen as drawing us 'into the
already existing relationship of the Father and the Son'. He is
alert to the dangers of a Spirit theology that is interested
'above all in the special effects department', forgetting that
'what the Spirit shapes is Jesus-like'. But he also lays stress on
the 'immense blessing' that the Charismatic movement has
brought, both to the Church and to him personally.

Returning to the historical record, Williams draws
attention to the dilemma faced by early Christians, especially
perhaps in the first two centuries, who wanted to do justice
to the biblical record, but were unsure how the Holy Spirit

fitted in. Irenaeus (*c.* 130–*c.* 200) is held to be an important exception, because he spoke of Son and Spirit as the two 'hands' of the Father moulding the world to the likeness of his glory. Origen (*c.* 185–*c.* 254), too, is singled out by Williams for the depth of his writing on so-called pneumatology. But the subject was neglected for much of the patristic era. Serious controversy about the Spirit erupted only in the later fourth century, after which 'subordinationist' views were rejected when the Spirit's full divinity was affirmed in the Nicene-Constantinopolitan creed of 381. Williams quotes the letters of Athanasius (*c.* 296–373) to his friend Serapion as a classic statement of the orthodox position: the Spirit does what God does – creating, renewing and sanctifying – and so should be called God as well.

From here we are led to consider how metaphysical theorising of this kind coheres with what has already been said about the First and Second Persons of the Trinity. Williams' argument is that if we were to talk about God only as Father and Son, we would be led to picture a static reflection: 'two just looking at each other, what the French call *égoïsme à deux*'. Language about the Holy Spirit arises because of a need to say that there is more than just that mirroring in God:

> there is an excess and a flow of love always and eternally more than just that correspondence, that reciprocity. And it's because of that that a world can appear that may be drawn into the life of Father and Son. God is eternally open to the world joining him. That's part of what the doctrine of the Holy Spirit says. God is eternally open to a world joining in his life.

For Williams, it follows from this that 'when the Son loves

the Father, he loves one who loves another . . . [he] doesn't simply love in a reciprocal, mirroring way, but loves the Father who breathes out the Spirit.' Grasp the fact that the Father always gives more than the mirror image that is the Son, and you realise that the relation of Father and Son can only be depicted 'by referring sideways to the Spirit', and thus to a triangulated reality. The trinitarian life is always 'a pointing away and a giving away', a notion held by Williams to be paralleled in our own experience. Healthy love between two persons 'is a love of the other's loving in general, not just their love for us'.

What gives grounds for belief in the Spirit is also what necessitates a community such as the Church, dedicated (in theory) to self-giving love: 'We have to be liberated from love for a God who just loves me or loves us,' Williams maintains.

> Augustine says that's the beginning of a real Christian sense of justice: to love the God who loves them, and therefore to be content that what I ask from God for myself I ask simultaneously for the other that God loves . . . the God who also loves Ian Paisley.

And if this is granted, then an orthodox theology will want to stress the way in which the Trinity 'makes possible, challenges, judges and transforms our life as community all the time'.

Williams emphasises the part played by the sacraments when he spells out the ways in which the Spirit is at work in the Church. Mindful of the relative neglect of the Spirit in Western theologies and Eucharistic rites, he focuses on the words of institution in the Orthodox Liturgy, which 'bring us to the contemporary reality of Jesus' in an especially resonant way. 'And when the Holy Spirit comes down on the gifts we put on the table . . . what happens, of course, is that bread becomes the common body, the life for all, the sign precisely of the God who doesn't just love me.' So to receive communion is to do trinitarian theology, whether or not one is aware of it. By taking part in the Eucharist,

> you are claiming your right as a baptised person to speak in the presence and power of Jesus Christ to the Father. You are coming to stand where Christ stood and stands, before the everlasting, generous source of all things. And you're doing it not because you're a successful spiritual adept . . . [but] because the right given you in baptism is the gift of the presence of the Spirit, to make you always contemporary with Jesus Christ.

Chapter Three

SPIRITUALITY

WILLIAMS IS PROBABLY KNOWN by more people as a spiritual guide than as a theologian: his sermons have reached a far broader audience than his academic works. As we have seen, his strategy involves reminting centuries-old material that appears stale or irrelevant to many. His *Teresa of Avila* (1991; reissued in 2000 by Continuum), a study of the great Spanish Carmelite, is a case in point. This chapter will outline Williams' less noticed ideas about three other sources of this kind – the sayings of the Desert Fathers,[1] the Dark Night of the Soul,[2] and praying with icons of Mary – and how they can assist in refining prayer and action.

The Desert Fathers (and Mothers) are separated from us by a large historical gulf. Their communities sprang up across the wildernesses of Egypt and Syria in reaction to materialism in the fourth-century Church. So the claim that their message remains apposite might seem especially hard to justify. Figures such as St Antony the Great (d. 356), father of Christian monasticism, Abbas Moses and Arsenius, and Amma Syncletica are usually associated with mystical prayer and extreme self-denial. But their writings make clear that they do not consider contemplation to be an end in itself. As

Williams says, 'it is the fruit and the source of a renewed style of living together.' Asceticism 'is not self-punishment, but a way of opening the eyes.' These monks and nuns lived in groups, or sometimes in solitude, to understand their humanity and 'to rediscover what it was that the Church was there for'. A large part of Williams' account of them derives from three sayings on this theme. Two come from St Antony: 'Our life and our death is with our neighbour' and 'if we gain our brother, we have gained God.' The third comes in a letter from Abba Moses the Egyptian to Abba Poemen: 'The monk must die to his neighbour and never judge him at all in any way whatever.'

Gaining a neighbour means putting him or her in touch with God, argues Williams. What can surprise the modern reader is the Desert Fathers' sense of the obstacles we put between other people and God. They saw that we are regularly undone by a form of inattention – the failure to see what other people really are – which in turn gives rise to inappropriate forms of harshness. There is much in the writings of the Desert Fathers about being harsh on harshness, Williams tells us, and about their view that we 'can read a good deal of the history of the Church as a sustained attempt to police one another's relationships with God on the part of Christian people'.

He illustrates this with a story about Macarius the Great, who lived at Skitis in the fifth century, and was thought to be very holy by dint of his unerring sense of divine mercy. He once visited another monk called Theopemptus. When they were alone, the old man asked Theopemptus how things were going. 'Thanks to your prayers, fine,' came the answer. 'Do your fantasies war against you?' the old man asked. 'No, up

till now it's all right,' answered Theopemptus, because he was
frightened of admitting the truth. 'Many years I've lived as an
ascetic,' said Macarius, 'and everybody praises me, but
though I'm an old man, I still have a lot of trouble with sexual fantasy.' Theopemptus replied: 'Well actually, Father, it's
the same with me.' Macarius went on to confess that one or
other form of temptation continued to affect him, until by
stages he brought Theopemptus to admit them all as well.
Then the old man asked the younger monk how long he spent
fasting. 'Till the ninth hour,' came the reply. 'Fast a little bit
longer,' Macarius said. 'Meditate on the gospel and the rest of
the Bible. If some alien thought arises within you, don't look
straight at it but look upwards. The Lord will come to your
help.'

Macarius' technique involves putting himself on the same
level as those he is counselling. In diagnosing his own
weakness, he induces Theopemptus to admit self-deceit.
'Inattention to the reality of the other leads to harshness,'
Williams infers. Harshness is linked to superiority.
Superiority induces moral blindness. And all these failures
cause despair or mistrust, which is the worst thing you can
possibly do in relation to anyone else. 'That's why dying to
the neighbour is about living with the neighbour.'

In this connection Williams quotes a saying of Abba John
the Dwarf: 'You don't build a house by beginning with the
roof and working down, you begin with the foundation . . .
The foundation is our neighbour whom we must win. That is
the place to begin. Every commandment of Christ depends
on this one.' It isn't a question of downplaying the seriousness
of sin, Williams argues: we habitually picture strenuousness
and relaxation as opposed qualities, but the Desert Fathers

resist that mould. They understand that 'failure is only healed by humility and solidarity, and not by condemnation.'

The fruits of such action are a fresh understanding of terms such as 'life' and 'gain'. Life involves 'being free to let God give through you'; this means that 'success' in the spiritual life is all to do with 'whether we are able to connect someone else with reconciliation and wholeness'. There is an obvious lesson here for the conduct of disputes in the Church. To see my triumph as another's loss is anti-Christian. If we must employ the 'more or less useless' vocabulary of success and failure, Williams urges, should we not think of the health of the Christian community 'in terms of our ability or otherwise . . . to connect one another with the wellsprings of reconciliation?'

<hr />

He hears contemporary echoes of the Desert Fathers in the work of philosophers such as Simone Weil and Iris Murdoch. They are united by opposition to a model of morality that involves the imposition of patterns on our environment through the blunt exercise of will. 'We live in a world where self-discovery and self-expression sound absolutely wonderful,' Williams observes wryly. 'If only everybody would go away, if only everybody else would stop telling me what to do, then I'd be so marvellous. Then my self would flower wonderfully in all its beauty and complexity.' But self-seeking motivations (above all, perhaps, the urge for self-justification) rage within us. And while we remain on the level of the will and the ego, 'we are not yet in touch with the truth of our being.'

He notes that religion is sometimes considered a good thing in contemporary society because it is seen as another consumer choice, and choice is held to be good for its own sake. The idea that religious belief represents 'labour, patience and pain', and that believers are seeking 'to allow truth to impinge', has faded from the picture. But as well as being individualist, we are also conformist, because choice is in fact managed for us with sharp efficiency by a vast system of consumer provision: 'Maximising the choice means in fact maximising the products that someone is designing for you, and that means at the end of the day that our choices are always and already channelled into conformist patterns.'

This in turn derives from a notion of personhood that is at odds with Christian (especially Eastern Orthodox) models. For Vladimir Lossky, the individual is just a bit of nature, not a person. An individual is just one instance of a general phenomenon. 'And the mysterious thing about human will and human choice is that actually it can be the least personal thing about us,' Williams thinks. Deep down, as he has frequently contended in other contexts, morality has less to do with a supermarket model of choice than with the education of desire. Whoever 'really has matured as a person, not as an individual, is perhaps the person who thinks least about choice'. Think of Jesus in the Garden of Gethsemane. Could he have fled? Did he really face the same kind of agony that we might face in a similar situation? In the Christian understanding, he could have made a different choice. But there was also a deeper sense in which he had no option, because of who he was. As Williams summarises it, 'the choice to betray would have been a violation of everything that he was, a tearing of the very fabric of his being.'

A parallel can be seen here with Edith Stein, the Jewish Carmelite murdered at Auschwitz. Arrested by a Nazi officer who greeted her by saying '*Heil Hitler*', she replied, '*Laudetur Jesus Christus*' (Jesus Christ be praised). This is what Williams means by 'that place beyond consumer freedom' reached by the saint. 'You don't have to think about it. You have become habituated to seeing and responding truthfully.' Such an idea of personhood could do wonders for the Church, he concludes, for a body of persons in relation will be free from 'the burden of self-justification' and thereby marked by far deeper maturity and charity than a body of 'mere individuals'.

Much Christian spiritual writing (including liturgy and hymnody) deals with heights and depths, feeding the idea that we are perpetually poised between salvation and the abyss. These days, of course, those who aren't frightened by language of this kind are more likely to mock it. Williams' lecture 'Staying' (on the Desert Fathers' idea of stability) tackles this question. He draws on Evagrius of Pontus (346–99), who reflects in detail on the problem of *acedia* or *accidie* – the sluggishness and melancholy that arise from boredom.

Williams glosses Evagrius' picture of the unappealing conditions a monk may face. 'You are on your own in the cell, time is dragging, it's a long time since breakfast. Is this life really worthwhile? It doesn't feel very holy.' All sorts of thoughts crowd in. You could visit another brother who would love to see you. You could go off to Alexandria to serve the poor and win a great reputation for charity. You could . . . 'And the hours move on, and the sun rises higher in the sky, and Evagrius with great perception identifies a feeling which, I guess, is known to all of us in varying degrees in the routine of our lives. How do we stay with ourselves?'

The Desert Fathers have plenty to say on the subject. Williams quotes the advice of an old man advising a restless younger monk. 'Go, eat, drink and sleep, but don't leave your cell. You must realise that it is endurance in the cell that leads the monk to his full stature.' The records say that the monk did this for three days, and then began to suffer boredom. So he found some palm leaves and trimmed them, and later began to plait them. Afterwards he had something to eat before finishing with the palm leaves. Then he read a little and chanted some psalms. 'And so, by the help of God, he advanced little by little till he reached his full stature.'

In other words, holiness is often prosaic: it consists in doing the next thing. Williams warns that 'we like to be noticed'. We would 'like our lives to be dramatic, to speak in compelling ways, and here are the Desert Fathers saying to us: eat, sleep, drink, plait a few leaves. Or whatever the equivalent is in your domestic situation.' To follow this advice is to take a step along the way of self-acceptance – to 'being committed to who you are', or, as an anonymous desert monk writes, 'pledging your body to a given place.'

The reverse of this is the fantasy of always wanting to be elsewhere or to transform one's circumstances; its *reductio ad absurdum* is Satan's preference for being in control of an illusory world over not being in control of a real one. And while 'pledging the body' (or 'the real, material self', in Williams' expression) invariably applies to the cell or the community for the desert monks, it means much else besides, including fidelity in marriage or friendship or prayer.

Williams notes that wealth and mobility have not made self-acceptance of this kind any easier to achieve. If anything, we are more restless than ever. Among the trends that disturb him are

> the passionate hunger for sexual variety, the con-
> sumerisation of area after area of our lives, the sense of
> the body as something on which the will can be
> inscribed, the fascination with style as an easily shifted
> set of clothes that can be put on and discarded, the
> impatience that we have these days with process.

He denies that the Desert Fathers are thereby consigning us to 'the wrong kind of passivity'. Much of their advice is about how a monk or nun can adjust his or her circumstances when a given pattern of life has stopped working. But his core point is that Christians should be examples of self-acceptance to those around them:

> So often people imagine that religious faith of various
> kinds represents a deep restlessness and refusal of the
> natural, the ordinary. And yet again and again in the
> great religious traditions it seems that we are drawn
> back to this challenge: can I be gratefully and accept-
> ingly who and what I am? . . . Only in the body is the
> soul saved . . . only in the body does healing happen . . .
> [the spiritual life is] responding to the particularity of
> the neighbour, the neighbour who is part of this
> inescapable material environment which I must love
> and recognise. There are no abstract neighbours.

The Christian will also face periods of longer and deeper spiritual aridity. Like many others, Williams finds an especi-ally penetrating account of difficulties with prayer in John of the Cross (1542–91), whose writings he calls 'a touchstone of authenticity' in this area. John lived in troubled times. He was imprisoned in Avila at the behest of the Inquisition for championing reforms to his Carmelite Order, but nevertheless earned fame as an exceptionally discerning spiritual director. His greatest poetic work, the *Songs of the Soul in Rapture*, represents the union between the soul and Christ in terms of a nocturnal elopement. It displays both technical brilliance – especially through rhythm and protracted rhyme schemes – and a level of erotic imagery that even modern readers find startling. Williams expounds the verse with assurance (he has a working knowledge of Spanish, besides his poetic credentials) before bringing theological instruments to a discussion of *The Ascent of Mount Carmel* and *The Dark Night of the Soul*, John's prose meditations on the *Songs*.

Behind these works lies a psychological blueprint inherited from Augustine: that human persons are distinguished by three capacities – memory, understanding and love (or will). Memory is the foundation of human life; we understand the world by absorbing its otherness; and we have attitudes towards things, we have a will towards things, and we love them. The snag is that each of these faculties is attached to the wrong kinds of target. Our memory and understanding are bound to a vain and self-serving picture of our current lives and past selves, and our love is channelled in many of the wrong places. Each faculty needs to be unpeeled from the objects to which it is usually attached, and to find a new goal in God. What is bad, on this view, is not the world as such, but our tendency to 'fall upon it' in a possessive way, so that we are snared by what we desire. Like the boy in Aesop's fable, 'we thrust our hand into the jar, fill it with nuts and can't pull it out, because our fists are clenched on the objects that we're after.'

The function of *The Ascent of Mount Carmel* and *The Dark Night of the Soul* is to describe the redirecting of our desires – a process that we can encourage in part by learning to let go and by ascetical practices (the so-called Active Night), but in which 'the real work is done by God'. Williams describes this stage (termed the Passive Night) as follows:

> God will see to it by his action in our minds and hearts that we are peeled away from our attachment to ideas of him and ideas of ourselves. God will see to it that we are left with no idols to worship. And that's where the life of the believer is meant to be difficult, and that's where the cross marks us most deeply. That is where, if you like, baptism begins to bite. It means, and [John] is painfully explicit about this, that most of your confident ideas about God will at some point cease to mean any-thing to you. They will just go dry. And the corollary of that is of course that your ideas about yourself go dry and dead. So you think you're doing well, you think you're a spiritual person: God is going to tell you different.

The Passive Night forms much of the subject matter of *The Dark Night of the Soul*, a document that has influenced Williams' spirituality in a profound way. A sermon he preached on the subject[3] makes clear his view of how the Dark Night sweeps all human religious constructions – con-servative, radical or whatever – away. If I am conservative, he says, my 'circular path' will consist in sacramental observance and a picture that sees God as 'the reliable source of meaning behind it all'. If I am radical, my God will disturb the social order with his call for a 'new and liberated humanity'.[4] But as they stand, Williams warns, both these pictures are illusions. 'They are, equally, religious games', which give credence to the atheist's charge that religion is a matter of wish-fulfilment. The only solid defence religion has against this accusation is the Dark Night – not understood as some kind of exalted experience, but as the reverse: the 'evacuation' of meaning. 'Suddenly we see that our path goes round a hole, a bottomless black pit. In the middle of all our religious constructs – if we have the honesty to look at it – is an emptiness. The Dark Night is God's attack on religion.'[5]

Far from giving up, though, the discerning Christian will see this as a crucial, positive stage:

> If you can accept and even rejoice in the experience of darkness, if you can accept that God is more than an idea which keeps your religion or philosophy or politics tidy – then you may find a way back to religion . . . that is more creative because you are more aware of the . . . uncontrollable quality of the truth at the heart of all things.[6]

John speaks of being suspended in mid-air at this stage, neither knowing where he is, nor what he is doing. But midnight is when it starts getting light. The darkest moment of dispossession is a positive stage, for it can herald the time when God becomes the object of our memory, understanding and love. Yoking these three activities to the three theological virtues of faith, hope and love, John speaks of the process as being about how memory turns into hope, understanding turns into faith, and will turns into love. 'It's not just a conceptual pattern,' Williams says:

> It's about how memory, instead of being preoccupied
> with an imprisoning past, becomes an absolute trust
> and openness to God's future. It's about how under-
> standing, instead of being a search for possessing and
> controlling the world around us, becomes again a loving
> trust and receptivity. It's about how will, the projection
> of our energy on to the world, becomes a love which is
> bonded with the very love of God.

So Williams usually gravitates towards a rhetoric of
humility and dispossession. He sees complacency and
acquisitiveness all around, and a carelessness about the language of faith among Christians that provides endless scope
for self-delusion and spiritual infantilism. Is this emphasis
carried too far? He is far too well versed in spiritual literature
not to see the danger in the wrong kind of humility. In
'"Know Thyself": What Sort of Injunction?',[7] an essay partly
devoted to this subject, he says that both black and feminist
theologies 'have often interpreted the summons to
repentance, provisionality, the unmasking of pride, as
inappropriate as addressed to them, as ideological
commendations of passivity in an intolerable situation'.[8] But
against this, he warns that 'the language of the victim can
become sterile and collusive. The personal is not the political
if it stops at being a programme of negation and the
reinstatement of the injured ego.'[9]

This sort of situation calls for sharp pastoral instincts. If we
ask how self-knowledge in others might be gauged, says
Williams,

it looks as if the answer might lie in trying to deal with questions like, 'Is there a pattern of behaviour here suggesting an unwillingness to learn or to be enlarged?' or 'Is there an obsessive quality to acts of self-presentation (in speech especially) that would indicate a fixed and defended image of needs that must be met for this self to sustain its position or power?'[10]

Nevertheless, the line between humility and self-suppression is thin, and Jesus speaks with different voices about the cost of discipleship (cf. Mt 11:28-30 and Mk 13:12-13). But Williams has a less rigorist side, especially in pastoral contexts. A taste of this style comes in his small book on icons, *Ponder These Things*.

It begins with a section on the *Hodegetria* (The One Who Points the Way), which gives early notice of the sophisticated theology at work in apparently simple images. We call something holy because it is a 'transitional space, a borderland, where the completely foreign is brought together with the familiar', and so an icon's holiness derives from its being 'so constructed as to open the world to the "energy" of God at work in what is being shown'.[11] People who pray with icons are led by faith 'both to live in the world' and 'to be aware of the utter strangeness of God that waits in the heart of what is familiar'.[12]

The *Hodegetria* depicts the Christ-child gazing at his mother and enfolded by her left arm. She points towards him with her right hand. We the viewers are thus drawn into a circular movement. Jesus' eyes lead us up to the Virgin, and her eyes are turned towards us. It is typical of much iconography to present us with persons in relation, not with solitary portraits, Williams comments. 'Mary is who she is by pointing away from herself: her identity is caught up in leading us to Jesus.'[13] But the Jesus we contemplate is not an isolated figure. He is consumed with 'loving attention' towards someone else. The image is making the substantial point that we are formed by our relations with others, and that we gain our lives by losing them.

The *Eleousa* (Virgin of Loving Kindness) icon goes further. Christ embraces Mary cheek to cheek, his hands clutching her neck and his foot thrust outwards. The scene may recall the Song of Songs 2:6 ('his left hand is beneath my head, and with his right hand he embraces me'). It tells us not just about a pattern of love, as in the *Hodegetria*, but about the 'intensity and immediacy' of that love. As we have seen, Williams believes that a great deal of spirituality begins with mistaken notions. For those who assume that God stands at a distance waiting for us to make a move in his direction, the *Eleousa* image should give us something of a shock. The Lord 'does not wait, impassive, as we babble on about our shame and penitence. His love is instead that of an eager and rather boisterous child.'[14] The theological lesson of this is linked to the conviction that God is closer to us than we are to ourselves. As Williams puts it:

> In human experience, intrusive or invasive love is an attempt to destroy something, the essential distance between person and person that makes human love a joyful and risky exploration of another's mysteriousness . . . But God's love for us does not face that kind of boundary, since God is not in any way another individual in competition with us. God simply is present to every

aspect of our being because he is its source and sustaining energy . . . As in the *Hodegetria*, Mary is the sign of our humanity engaged by God. But if the *Hodegetria* is more obviously about Mary as the type of the disciple and witness, [in the *Eleousa*] the reference is broadened out: Mary is creation itself embraced by Christ, and more specifically human creation, invaded by Christ and disoriented, disarranged by his coming.[15]

In Williams' interpretation, the *Orans* (the Virgin of the Sign) is one of the most suggestive icons ever produced. From the earliest times, the Church was represented symbolically as a woman, and the *Orans* figure (a woman praying with hands extended) stood for the whole believing community considered as Christ's bride. In the icon inspired by this model, Christ is shown praying inside Mary, reminding us that for the nine months of her pregnancy, 'the presence of God incarnate in the world was not in visible action or speech, but wholly in secrecy.'[16]

The first lesson to flow from this is that the *Orans* (like icons generally) has an ecclesiological function: in the Church, human nature is 'restored and transfigured' by divine grace. At the same time, Christian fellowship

> is nothing less than Christ's reality, and thus Christ's action – the ceaseless movement towards the Father that is the life of the eternal Son, responding to the outflowing of the Father's life which generates it. The trinitarian pulse is the heartbeat of the Church.[17]

But Jesus' hiddenness in the icon should temper our urge to define the body of his followers too narrowly. A moment of 'desperately needy openness to God on the part of very irregular Christians' might fuel the Church just as much as 'the routine prayer of the worshipping community'.[18] Our instinct is to think that God operates in us 'at the points where we sense we are on the right lines, not those areas of our life where we feel at sea'.[19]

Two further insights follow from this. The first (as we have also seen with John of the Cross) is that God in Christ may be most real 'in the lonely dryness of a prayer that seems to be going nowhere', and, second, that the Church needs neither to be constantly reassuring itself of its success and purity, nor to be too preoccupied with 'pinning down where the centre is'. Since Christ himself is its living centre, the Church can shun idolatry and 'stay with the mysteriousness of Christ's presence rather than creating an accessible but false picture to hang on to'.[20]

Chapter Four

+⊱⊰+

POLITICS

POLITICS AND ECONOMICS are not Williams' areas of professional expertise, and weightier voices have been raised against him in these fields than elsewhere. Dissenting views will therefore be reported at greater length in this chapter. As I have suggested, he is more plain-spoken about politics than about theology. But there are continuities that bear repeating at this stage — above all, the manner in which Williams derives his allegiance to socialism from doctrinal premisses. He stands on the same ground as the late David Nicholls, another Anglican left-winger, who asked whether

> we can even understand the idea of God as Trinity — a community in which 'none is afore, or none after: none is greater or less than another' — unless we have had some experience of co-operation and community in our social and political life. If for no other reason, those who are anxious about doctrinal orthodoxy ought to be troubled about political structures.[1]

So it is the creed itself that gives rise to demands for a shift in the balance of wealth. Christians who take up this line of thinking will be drawn to a pre-Blair Labour agenda, Williams thinks, or, better still, to the ethos of the traditional Independent Labour Party: supportive of state ownership in industry, 'sympathetic to pacifism, internationalist in style but not too keen on the corporatism of pro-Europeans . . . with powerful redistributive tendencies where taxation is concerned'.[2] They will give a high priority to Green issues, and are likely to think that 'lifestyle' is 'a question about your consumption of energy and ideologically sound coffee rather than your sexual preferences and interior decoration.'[3]

Williams sets out the theoretical basis for these beliefs in 'Liberation Theology and the Anglican Tradition' (1983),[4] an essay written for the Inter-Anglican Theological and Doctrinal Commission. It starts by rehearsing the case for a political dimension to discipleship. Since faith brings Christians into new patterns of relation centred on the memory and presence of Jesus, the Church's mission should obviously involve a survey of what impedes this process. The agenda will include engagement with the social sciences and other disciplines: to resist this encounter would be 'to retreat to a theological absolutism which effectively imprisons the gospel and blocks its communication'.[5]

The 1980s saw a deep conflict among Roman Catholics over the viability of employing Marxist categories in the fight for justice in Latin America. Several theologians were accused by the Vatican of polluting Christian doctrine with alien ideology. Rome in turn faced a similar counter-charge – that by rejecting as political only what challenged the current order, it was expressing an unacknowledged secular agenda of its own. Williams is well aware of the complexities involved here, yet he is certain that liberation theologies are genuinely anchored in the assumptions behind any serious

preaching of the gospel. A classic work such as Gustavo
Gutiérrez's *A Theology of Liberation* (SCM Press, 1974)
reminds us that theology is not a politically neutral or innocent enterprise. Like all intellectual systems, 'it is in fact
operating in somebody's interest, and so long as it is blind to
this truth it will operate in the interests of the status quo
(because it is in the interest of the status quo not to be questioned and relativised).'[6] As revolutionary awareness
develops in societies affected by acute conflict, the Church
will be faced by the question of whose interests it is serving.
The answer of liberation theology is a commitment to the
poor and powerless – practically, through charitable and
political action; intellectually, through exposition of the relevant corroborative texts in the Bible and tradition. A theology of liberation will thereby secure the liberation of
theology, as Juan Luis Segundo, another major figure, has
suggested.

Segundo believes that this course must be influenced by
Marxism to some degree, because it is to Marx that we owe
our awareness of 'the interests served by ideological constructs'.[7] Theological statements may indeed be relativised as
a result, but this is not a drawback in liberationist eyes,
because all theologies are relative to their context. What
matters is that theologians should be aware of this, and honest about whose side they are on. As Williams summarises it:
'Theological certainty is inseparable from commitment to a
particular human project; theological truth is inseparable
from the durability of that project. There is no other kind of
absoluteness in our history.'[8]

So he is much more sympathetic to Gutiérrez's estimate
of liberation theology than to Cardinal Ratzinger's: 'Where

the practical drive towards a "renewed humanity" or a freer society is concretely bound to Marxist-inspired political action, opting for a particular view of the human project will involve choices for or against Marxism.'[9] This need not involve confusing the Kingdom of God with a Marxist utopia, because the so-called base communities that have grown up in Latin America are nothing like the manipulative elite conceived in Leninist ideology. One reason for this springs from Christian belief in the sacraments, seen (in Lionel Thornton's words) as 'prophetic symbols of a transformed creation, as well as the fundamental means through which the process of transformation is normally effected'.[10] Following Segundo, Williams defines the task of the base community as 'the consistent living out of a radical, inevitably political, but also reflective, prayerful and sacramentally oriented Christian discipleship'.[11] This vision 'of possible futures in an unfree present' would not, he thinks, be shared by orthodox Marxists. What is more, it goes beyond the 'sterile' alternatives of individual liberty and mass collectivism, by picturing the Church as an intermediate structure between individuals or smaller units of society and the State. More broadly, the liberationist vision is not of the full realisation of the Kingdom of God in history; it is more concerned with challenging 'patterns of power and dominance, in the effort to push the mechanisms of mass society towards operating in favour of the disadvantaged.'[12]

While conceding that a 'consistent theory' of the relation of Church to society has not yet been worked out – and that the situations in Britain and Latin America diverge sharply – Williams holds that the liberationist gospel can still flower in

Anglican soil. He accepts that after breaking with Rome, the Church of England allied itself 'with a theory of absolute sovereign right vested in the monarch and the state apparatus'.[13] Thus theological reflection on religion and politics assumed what David Nicholls and others have termed an 'incarnationalist' slant. Nicholls sees this as 'generally optimistic and gradualist', believing that God's Kingdom will come 'slowly, silently and peacefully, and that the mighty will be lowered so gently from their seats as not to feel the bump when they reach the ground'.[14] Incarnationalists tend to sacralise the existing order. They may be paternalistic, believing that there are no basic conflicts of interest in the nation, and that the common good can be realised 'if people would behave a bit more reasonably'. Nicholls contrasts this with the 'redemptionist' model of Church–State relations. This accepts the underlying goodness of the created order, but emphasises the radical implications of the Fall:

> It sees the purpose of God in Christ as the ultimate reconciliation of all things, yet insists that the death of Christ on the cross represents the mortal battle between the forces of good and evil in the universe (cf. Ephesians 6:12) . . . For redemptionists the message of Christ's kingdom desacralises every human institution . . . even the Church must not be seen as an end in itself but as a symbol and means for the realisation of the heavenly city.[15]

Prominent exponents of the incarnationalist approach include theologians such as F. D. Maurice (1805–72), whose political thought Williams finds hopelessly compromised. Redemptionism developed more strongly within the Church of England early in the twentieth century. As one might expect, Williams thinks it provides a securer basis for theological radicalism, even though the two models are not mutually exclusive, and his faith in socialist strategies sometimes reflects an incarnationalist optimism. He draws especially on the thought of J. N. Figgis (1866–1919), a member of the Mirfield community, to propose an Anglican political strategy with more grit than Maurice's. Figgis traced the State's powers of religious coercion to an attempt by Renaissance and early modern secular rulers to lay hold of the absolute sovereignty formerly claimed by popes. But this coercion could operate only in religiously monolithic societies. Given the fact of toleration for the Free Churches in Britain, the only ground on which the Church of England could justify its own existence was by what Williams describes as a 'federalist' theory of ecclesiastical unity and authority. It follows that

> we cannot consistently be federalists in our ecclesiology and absolutists in our politics. It might even be said that the Anglican has a peculiarly direct reason for adopting a strongly syndicalist view of political power and the rights of associations over against an encroaching state.[16]

Figgis has little to say about economics, but Williams finds no underlying contradiction between the Mirfield man's view and 'Marx's insistence that the state must in some circumstances be administered on behalf of the proletariat, to rectify the imbalance of interest in bourgeois society.'[17] And he thinks that this can be accepted even by Christians who are sceptical about Marx's forecasts of the withering away of the

State, or who think that 'the idea of the dictatorship of the proletariat will need some qualification'.[18]

+►—◄+

While not merely political, then – 'not functional to some other and limited version of human destiny' – the gospel raises the most fundamental political questions. For their part, Jesus and his contemporaries would have been familiar with the Old Testament notion of jubilee, where economic inequalities were rectified every few years. In an essay on poverty also written in the 1980s, Williams yokes this to a contemporary socialist agenda:

> If we say . . . that only a socialist party can build in the kind of public accountability and self-critical candour that such a reviewing process demands, this is not to *identify* the gospel with socialism, nor to pretend that we have had any particularly impressive workings of it out in this or in any other European state this century. It is, though, to admit that only some such practice offers long-term hope for the poor . . . and if my argument is at all reasonable, this hope is intimately bound up with the hope for a new humanity that can understand and love and value itself in the light of nothing less than God.[19]

Williams' presidential address to the Bevan Foundation's 2002 Annual General Meeting is a snapshot of how his thinking had evolved over fifteen years. As in his Dimbleby Lecture several months later, he draws on the thought of Philip Bobbitt, once an adviser to President Clinton, who holds that globalisation is preventing the nation state from controlling its economy and currency. Since governments can no longer do what was once expected of them within fixed territorial boundaries, they are facing a crisis of political legitimacy. Bobbitt argues that their way of addressing this is through the emergence of the 'market state', in which a government's legitimacy is tied up with maximising the opportunities of its citizens. As Williams sees it, 'the point of government is not to protect and secure a relatively prosperous corporate identity but to clear the decks for opportunity.'[20] He finds this worrying not because the clock can be turned back and globalisation somehow abolished, but because governments are applying the vocabulary and mechanisms of the market in inappropriate areas, such as health and education. More generally, the market focus is deemed to be too individualist: 'if we are moving towards the market state, we [should] be thinking about a legitimacy . . . that will maximise opportunities for communities rather than for individuals.'

Although some of the Bevan Foundation's literature includes social wish lists with which scarcely anyone would quarrel, Williams and his colleagues have achieved practical results in the field that they term 'brokerage'. Community regeneration in areas of South Wales such as Ebbw Vale has been harmed by competitive bidding between statutory and voluntary bodies. Help has come from church people, among others, who 'facilitate conversation about common goals, conversation beyond competition, and ask about corporate needs and opportunities'. Vision of this kind need not rest on a big-government model of socialism. The basis can instead be 'that syndicalist vision, the community of communities, which allows a little bit more interplay between what the local community can identify and what the wider community can do to enable it'.[21]

Williams believes that a model of this kind is conducive to 'political virtue' as defined by the German theologian Ernst Wolff. This involves looking towards

> a state or form of governance which is prepared to defend its legitimacy, its right to be obeyed and accepted, in terms of its ability not to maximise opportunities to individuals but to maximise opportunities to communities; and to do so not just by providing an abstract set of goods that everybody can bid for, but by putting resources into the educational, regenerative work that is needed to assist communities in intelligent, conversational planning about their own good that will lead to a corporately owned set of goals.[22]

If the Bevan Foundation were to have a catchier title, Williams concludes, he would suggest calling it the Campaign for Real Politics.

+⊫━⊨+

Several features of the material described above help explain the mixed notices it has received. Much of it looks ageless – the thirst for justice, the concern about complacency, the underlying radical edge. Some of it is of its time, especially the sense that Marxism provides the great intellectual challenge to Church and society. It is heavily theoretical, grounded in a limited amount of practical experience, and perhaps reflects what one senior church official calls 'the neglect of applied theology in British universities'. This complaint is put more pointedly by David Martin, formerly Professor of Sociology at the London School of Economics:

> Rowan's arguments tend to sail on general ideas rather than on a concrete analysis of what politicians are actually able to do. He thinks that there's a division of labour: the church leader's job is to spell out principles, and the politician's job is to apply them. The trouble is that, as a result, the churchman is placing in the public domain elements that the politician can't always take on board.

Others, of course, consider Williams guilty of nothing more than taking the gospel seriously; and a further group feel confident that a more developed synthesis on a Christian input for public policy will emerge as he spends longer in the spotlight. His opinions are not static. Asked now about his attitude to capitalism, for example, he confesses that a change in his attitude is under way. The old antipathy had much to do with the manner in which the Thatcher reforms were introduced, he says. 'It was during the early 1980s that I joined the Labour Party for a time . . . Like many others, I didn't resist the temptation to take a pretty Manichaean view of what was going on.' Looking back at Britain's recent economic landscape, Williams accepts that he was slow to recognise the economic malaise which Tory reforms were designed to remedy. But he can still use strident language about the free market. In a Christian Socialist Movement pamphlet as recently as 1995, he writes that 'we have been encouraged to believe that competitiveness is all that matters – that is to say that my welfare can be secured without consideration of anyone else's.'[23] There are also traces of this view in *A Moral Society* (1996), a Churches Together in Wales document produced under Williams' chairmanship. One of its deepest complaints is about the alleged all-pervasiveness of competition in the public domain, and selfishness and short-term perspectives in private life.

Williams' critics tend to feel that his arguments skirt round an apparently uncomfortable reality – that high levels of public expenditure depend on thriving economies, which in turn rely on the cultivation of instincts that sit very awkwardly with gospel priorities. Is there a way out of this conundrum? An observer who has no hesitation in regarding the market as 'enormously important in the fulfilment of human needs and purposes' is John Kennedy, Co-ordinating Secretary for Church and Society at Churches Together in Britain and Ireland. Asked how this can be squared with the gospel's call to altruism, Kennedy draws inspiration from Adam Smith, who, he considers, has been unfairly identified with the 'vulgar and ruinous hotchpotch known as "Thatcherism"'.[24] The Great Society depicted in Book V of Smith's *The Wealth of Nations* 'is one in which people may balance their pursuit of self-interest with a pursuit of equality', Kennedy suggests. 'A society is blessed where the two impulses are optimised – where ambition and ingenuity and innovation in pursuit of self-improvement are balanced by an imaginative sympathy for the fate of others.'

Kennedy develops his argument in an article on the morality of wealth creation[25] which subverts the assumptions behind many documents on the subject published under church auspices. He suggests that

The market is not essentially exploitative. A growing market economy needs customers, and has no vested interest in their poverty. Quite the reverse – the butcher and the baker's interest tends to be served if their customers are prosperous. The market does not eliminate greed, ambition and vanity from the world, but it does compel the greedy and the ambitious to compete openly with others by lawful means . . . Markets do not especially hurt the poor. Wherever there are poor people, by definition whatever is going on has hurt them. It seems hardly necessary to say this, but so much Christian rhetoric is bound up in the notion that the market is alright for us, but not for them. This noble sentiment doesn't square with reality.[26]

Kennedy commends the so-called European model of political economy, based on the social market that transformed a country such as Germany during the decades after the Second World War. A more theological coda argues that Christian thinking about economics has been consistently impaired by a streak of puritanism:

The generation of widespread private prosperity which is then taxed at almost fifty per cent for the service of mainly peaceful public purposes seems to be a scheme not entirely without merit . . . It is false and blasphemous to celebrate any social order as a significant fulfilment of God's loving will. It follows, therefore, that it is pharisaical to denounce a society for not perfectly fulfilling that will, and this is a danger that elements of the Church topple into.[27]

Noting that 'some Christians are always creating more wealth for others to feel guilty about', he holds that the ascetic life is a calling (as, say, for John the Baptist), not something that can be imposed. 'To treat the whole world as a failed holy order is deeply mistaken. The ethic of the monastery made universal and compulsory ends in the Gulag.'[28] Kennedy is certainly not accusing Williams of such extremism; the argument has more to do with a possible confusion of ends and means. 'It is one thing to make the relief of poverty a priority,' Kennedy concludes,

> but another to think that only one kind of medicine will do. During the 1970s and 80s I observed varieties of old-style socialism in operation in Sri Lanka, Tower Hamlets [east London] and Nicaragua. The policies pursued in these three settings were not the best ways of helping the disadvantaged.

In the remainder of this chapter we shall look at a particular example – the case for and against economic globalisation – to get a sharper sense of the questions Williams has been confronting. His thoughts are set out in an address to a City audience of Christian executives in November 2001.[29] Early on he quotes the journalist John Lloyd's definition of globalisation as

> the creation of 24-hour markets, 24-hour instant communication, the opening of the world to financial markets, and the spread of the leisure-entertainment-news

industries almost to its every corner. It is also the huge expansion of transnational institutions such as the United Nations, the International Monetary Fund and the World Bank, the growth of non-governmental organisations and the creation of the anti-globalising movements themselves. All these overlap and depend on each other.

Williams then concedes that globalisation may sometimes operate benignly. The easy flow of capital means that local enterprise can be stimulated. Prosperity spreads, and education and democratic accountability spread with it. But the process entails big risks. 'The drainage of investment capital – which may be the result of many factors, not only failure on the ground – doesn't simply leave an economy where it was before. Earlier forms of economic activity may have become unsustainable; demographic patterns will have altered.' In this sort of instance, globalisation will have led to the growth of urban underclasses.

He illustrates this with the experience of a Thai woman whose plight was reported by the American writer Barbara Garson. An oil refinery in Thailand began to generate a service economy around it. The woman had moved from the country, where she worked on a farm, to a sweatshop making textiles near the refinery, and then to its gates to sell rice dishes. Later, the Thai currency fell sharply. The price of rice went up, the street vendor disappeared from the economy, and probably became part of a 'developing urban subproletariat'. She could not just go back to the paddy fields. For Williams (as for many exponents of Roman Catholic social teaching), this example is symptomatic of the way in which globalisation uncouples the economic and the social.

The lecture then draws attention to the fact that the principles of globalisation are contradicted by European and North American trade barriers that inhibit African development, and includes an example from South Wales – the closure of the Corus steel works – purporting to show how competition is regarded as good only when it suits business interests. When the shutting down of these plants was announced early in 2001, the suggestion of an employees' buyout was rejected by senior management through what was seen as a wish 'to pre-empt competition because of the vulnerable state of the international steel market'. Williams detects 'corporate doublespeak' in this decision: 'because of unavoidable competition, the workforce has to be reduced; but the company as such has to be protected from fresh competition.'

The address includes a plea for more Third World debt relief, and heavy criticism of the effects of World Bank structural adjustment programmes and of alleged inaction by American drug companies in sending cheap anti-retroviral drugs for AIDS patients in Africa. Turning to a list of positive suggestions, Williams commends Sergei Bulgakov's Christian socialist alternative to Marxism in early twentieth-century Russia. What Bulgakov principally opposed was 'the notion of an integrated, intelligible set of economic motivations that can be isolated from other human concerns. Economics is problem-solving; the definition of the problems can't be done by economics alone.' We cannot return to pre-modern systems of production. But 'if global economics is to work, it needs global institutions – which in turn requires unprecedentedly high levels of international co-operation and trust. And this is where, surely, the transnational Church, the universal citizens' assembly, convoked by God, can play its part.'

Praised in many and various church circles, the lecture drew clashing verdicts from economists. 'He doesn't seem aware of the misery that can also be caused by resistance to trade liberalisation,' said one. 'Currency stability depends on a country's productivity, its trade balance and its budget. Superficial currency stabilisation will not work.' Another expressed surprise that Williams had never acknowledged what other commentators took to be pivotal – that overall and despite its drawbacks, globalisation and/or free market reforms have helped to lift unprecedented numbers of people out of poverty in recent decades. Supporters of this view are not questioning the importance of helping casualties of the system. They are simply concerned that the territory may be mapped in misleading ways.

A defence of globalisation was made by Clive Crook, Deputy Editor of *The Economist*, in a lecture at St Paul's Cathedral in January 2003. In some ways his conclusions mirror those already sketched. Crook is no less eager than Williams is for a large boost in aid budgets, further debt relief, and the abolition of the trade barriers that the European Union imposes on Africa. He also judges the standard defence of globalisation to be inadequate. It is not inevitable: we are right to ask whether we want it and, if so, how we can improve it. The moral dimension is crucial. But he also maintains that many criticisms of globalisation are 'absurdly exaggerated'. Society should try to cushion the victims as much as possible, 'but in the end the morality of this process will inescapably come down to weighing what one hopes are the greater gains of the majority against the smaller losses of the unfortunate.' In comparison with pre-industrial times, he points out, people in the West live lives that are free from toil, disease and the fear of starvation. If change were ruled out merely by the existence of people adversely affected by it, then the Industrial Revolution itself would have been inadmissible.

Several more of Crook's arguments are worth noting in this context. One claim hallowed by frequent repetition is that the gap between rich and poor is widening ever more sharply. In 1999, for example, the United Nations Development Programme (UNDP) stated that the distance between the richest and poorest country was about 3 to 1 in 1820, 11 to 1 in 1913, 35 to 1 in 1950, 44 to 1 in 1973 and 72 to 1 in 1992. 'By the late 1990s, according to a UNDP document, the fifth of the world's people living in the highest-income countries had 86 per cent of the world's GDP – the bottom fifth just 1 per cent.' But Crook believes that this sort of comparison is seriously misleading, because the richest and poorest countries keep changing. The most impoverished nations in any given year will be those struck by short- or medium-term crises such as war, drought or political ferment. Spool on a decade, and the situation will almost certainly have altered.

Moreover, he maintains that ratios such as 86 to 1 are distorted because they take no account of the enormous varieties in the cost of living between poor and rich countries. Crook commends the more accurate reading provided by so-called Purchasing Power Parity (PPP). On this gauge, the ratio between the two shares was 13 to 1, not 86 to 1. In 1968, the ratio calculated in this way was 15 to 1. He concludes that 'possibly for the first time, global inequality *declined* in the two decades to the late 1990s.' There is no room for complacency, but 'we are nevertheless dealing with a problem which is tractable.' And by historical standards, 'the world is making remarkable progress on poverty,' especially in China and India, where most of the world's poor people live.

But Williams was praised for 'an above average non-specialist grasp of the problem' by the New Economics Foundation, a radical think-tank. Its Policy Director, Andrew Simms, considers PPP a flawed yardstick on several grounds. First, because dollars 'are an important measure in their own right'. Wherever poor countries have to engage with the global economy, they have to use dollars: to pay the service on their foreign debts, to conduct international trade, and to buy oil to run their domestic economies if they are energy importers. Second, while the percentage of the population in the least developed countries living on less than $2 a day 'has remained effectively static over the last 35 years ... the actual number of such poor people has more than doubled from 211 million to 449 million.' Above all, says Simms, the advancement of China and India has occurred 'not as a result of the free market model, trade and financial liberalisation as the core of the globalisers' agenda, but from doing their own thing'. He holds this to prove that 'if you want to get ahead as a poor country, the first thing you should do is tear up the neo-liberal rule book.'

The whole point is broadened out by Jessica Bridges Palmer, a colleague of Simms:

> It is true that absolute gaps between richer and poorer nations are misleading. What is more important in terms of the long-term sustainability and stability of life is the gap between the richest and poorest people on

earth, and it would be very difficult to argue by any sleight of statistics that this gap has not increased obscenely. More and more wealth is owned and resources consumed by fewer and fewer people – a transnational global elite held to account by no one but shareholders, and then only for the amount of wealth they can extract and return as interest. Globalisation as it is proceeding now has no medium of accountability that would address that inequality and ensure that increased aggregate wealth amounts to increased aggregate well-being. Inequality is both immoral and ultimately counter-productive – without a greater sharing of the wealth generated on the planet, progress, however it is defined, will always be depressingly finite.

<hr />

Arbitrating between Crook and the New Economic Foundation lies well beyond my remit. The point of quoting other verdicts in some detail here is to indicate that for Christians, the easy consensus warned against by Williams in other contexts is no less elusive in the political sphere. But whether one judges his brand of socialism to be prophetic or other-worldly (or just that economics is as inexact a science as theology), one doctrine underlying his contribution is not in dispute. As he said in his Canterbury enthronement sermon, 'Jesus' followers grieve or protest about war, debt, poverty and prejudice because of the fear we feel when insult and violence blot out the divine image in human relations.' And because of what this implies. For Catholic Christianity, pessimism about our brittle state is eclipsed by hope.

Notes

Introduction

1. Rowan Williams, 'Whatever happened to all the hope?, *Church Times*, 1 May 1998.
2. Rowan Williams, press conference, 23 July 2002.
3. David L. Edwards, 'From Wales – scholarship and spirituality', *Church Times*, 17 May 2002.
4. Epilogue in Christina Rees (ed.), *Voices of This Calling: Experiences of the First Generation of Women Priests* (Canterbury Press, 2002), p. 213.
5. Rowan Williams, *On Christian Theology* (Blackwell, 2000), p. 5.
6. ibid., p. 6.
7. ibid., p. xv.
8. Rowan Williams, 'Saving Time: Thoughts on Practice, Patience and Vision', *New Blackfriars*, June 1992, p. 321.
9. Rees, *Voices of This Calling*, p. 213.
10. ibid., p. 213.
11. Williams, *On Christian Theology*, p. xiii ff.
12. ibid., p. xv.

Chapter 1: Student, Scholar, Pastor

1. The comment comes from John Webster, Williams' successor as Lady Margaret Professor at Oxford.
2. Herbert McCabe, in David L. Edwards (ed.), *The Honest to God Debate* (SCM Press, 1963), p. 167.
3. ibid., p. 175.
4. Rowan Williams, 'Acting on God's behalf', *Church Times*, 14 March 1997.
5. Rowan Williams, in a lecture given to theology students in Cambridge, 2 March 2002.
6. Rowan Williams, *The Kingdom Is Theirs: Five Reflections on the Beatitudes* (Christian Socialist Movement, October 2002), p. 10.
7. Interview with Paul Handley, *Church Times*, 6 December 2002.
8. Rowan Williams, 'Eastern Orthodox Theology', in David F. Ford (ed.), *The Modern Theologians: An Introduction to Christian Theology in the Twentieth Century*

(Blackwell, 1989), Volume II, p. 153.

9. ibid., p. 161.

10. ibid., p. 161.

11. ibid., p. 161.

12. Rowan Williams, *The Poems of Rowan Williams* (Perpetua Press, 2002), p. 17.

13. Rowan Williams, *The Wound of Knowledge* (Darton, Longman and Todd, 1979), p. 182.

14. Rowan Williams, 'On Doing Theology' in Christina Baxter, Roger Greenacre and John R. W. Stott (eds.), *Stepping Stones: Joint Essays on Anglican Catholic and Evangelical Unity* (Hodder & Stoughton, 1987).

15. ibid., p. 4.

16. John Milbank, 'The Programme of Radical Orthodoxy' in Laurence Paul Hemming (ed.), *Radical Orthodoxy? A Catholic Enquiry* (Ashgate, 2000), p. 34.

17. Rowan Williams, *Resurrection: Interpreting the Easter Gospel* (Darton, Longman and Todd, 1982), p. 117.

18. ibid., p. 117.

19. ibid., p. 119.

20. ibid., p. 118.

21. Rupert Shortt, 'Profile of John Sweet', *Church Times*, 15 October 1993.

22. John Hick (ed.), *The Myth of God Incarnate* (SCM Press, 1977), p. 178.

23. Herbert McCabe, *God Matters* (Geoffrey Chapman, 1987), p. 57.

24. Rowan Williams, 'Doctrinal Criticism: Some Questions' in Sarah Coakley and David Pailin (eds.), *The Making and Remaking of Christian Doctrine: Essays in Honour of Maurice Wiles* (Clarendon, 1993).

25. See for example Maurice Wiles, *The Remaking of Christian Doctrine* (SCM Press, 1974).

26. Williams, 'Doctrinal Criticism: Some Questions', p. 255.

27. ibid., p. 256.

28. ibid., p. 257.

29. ibid., p. 260.

30. Rowan Williams, *The Truce of God* (Fount, 1983), p. 118.

31. ibid., pp. 55–6.

32. Oliver O'Donovan, 'Rowan Williams: The New Archbishop of Canterbury. A Symposium', *Pro Ecclesia*, Vol. XII No. 1, p. 6.

33. ibid., p. 6.

34. ibid., p. 6.

35. Alasdair MacIntyre, *After Virtue* (Duckworth, 1981), p. 206.

36. The Lesbian and Gay Christian Movement, Oxford House, Derbyshire Street, London E2 6HG.

37. 'The Body's Grace' (LGCM, 1989), p. 4.
38. ibid., p. 5.
39. ibid., p. 8.
40. *Desert Island Discs*, BBC Radio 4, 22 December 2002.
41. Densil Morgan, *The Span of the Cross* (University of Wales Press, 1999), p. 274.
42. ibid., p. 275.
43. Williams, *The Poems of Rowan Williams*, p. 46.
44. ibid., p. 8.
45. The text of the lecture can be obtained from the Anglican Communion website (www.anglicancommunion.org).
46. Williams, *The Poems of Rowan Williams*, p. 71.
47. Rowan Williams, *Writing in the Dust* (Hodder & Stoughton, 2002), p. 51.
48. ibid., p. 23.
49. ibid., p. 25.
50. Rowan Williams, 'Alternative Views: opinion formers speak out', *The Guardian*, 25 September 2002.
51. Interview with Paul Handley, *Church Times*, 6 December 2002.
52. ibid.
53. Williams, *The Poems of Rowan Williams*, p. 40.
54. A. N. Wilson, 'Canterbury finds itself a startling new voice', *The Daily Telegraph*, 12 December 2002.

Chapter 2: Philosophy and Theology

1. See for example Rowan Williams, 'Between Politics and Metaphysics: Reflections in the Wake of Gillian Rose', *Modern Theology,* January 1995.
2. Rowan Williams, 'Logic and Spirit in Hegel' in Philip Blond (ed.), *Post-Secular Philosophy* (Routledge, 1998), p. 119.
3. ibid., p. 121 ff.
4. Williams' text is available online in the archive of www.hayfestival.co.uk.
5. Samuel Taylor Coleridge, *On the Constitution of Church and State* (Dent, 1972), pp. 98–9.
6. See for example Matthew Parris, 'For God's sake, Archbishop, this isn't the State we're in', *The Times*, 21 December 2002.
7. Ferdinand Mount, 'Tony and the turbulent priest get serious', *The Sunday Times*, 29 December 2002.
8. Baxter, Greenacre and Stott (eds.), *Stepping Stones*, p. 2.
9. Unless otherwise indicated, all the quoted material on the incarnation and the Spirit is drawn from recordings of lectures on doctrine and spirituality that Williams gave to a Church Union audience in Bristol at intervals

between 1997 and 2002. Edited transcripts are due to be published at a future date.

10. Rowan Williams, 'No Life Here – no joy, terror or tears', *Church Times*, 17 July 1998.

11. Rowan Williams, 'The Cross in the 21st Century' in *Seven Words for the 21st Century* (Darton, Longman and Todd, 2002), p. 3.

12. ibid., p. 3.

13. ibid., p. 7.

Chapter 3: Spirituality

1. Unless otherwise indicated, my quotations are taken from transcripts of 'Spirit in the Desert', lectures Williams gave on prayer and meditation to the John Main Seminar in Sydney, Australia, in August 2001. They will also be published in due course.

2. Most of the quoted material on John of the Cross in this chapter comes from an address Williams gave to the Church Union in Bristol in January 2001.

3. Rowan Williams, *Open to Judgement* (Darton, Longman and Todd, 1994), p. 95 ff.

4. ibid., p. 95.

5. ibid., p. 97.

6. ibid., p. 97.

7. Rowan Williams, '"Know Thyself": What Sort of Injunction?' in Michael McGhee (ed.), *Philosophy, Religion and the Spiritual Life* (Cambridge University Press, 1992), p. 211 ff.

8. ibid., p. 224.

9. ibid., p. 225.

10. ibid., p. 225.

11. Rowan Williams, *Ponder These Things* (Canterbury Press, 2002), pp. xiv–xv.

12. ibid., p. xvii.

13. ibid., p. 7.

14. ibid., p. 23.

15. ibid., p. 33 ff.

16. ibid., p. 45.

17. ibid., p. 46.

18. ibid., p. 48.

19. ibid., pp. 49–50.

20. ibid., p. 55.

Chapter 4: Politics

1. David Nicholls, 'Two Tendencies in Anglo-Catholic Political Theology' (1983), in *Politics and Theological Identity* (Jubilee Group, 1984), pp. 41–2.
2. Rowan Williams, 'Is Blair still a Christian socialist?', *New Statesman*, 22 September 1998.
3. ibid.
4. Rowan Williams, 'Liberation Theology and the Anglican Tradition' (1983), in *Politics and Theological Identity*.
5. ibid., p. 10.
6. ibid., p. 11.
7. ibid., p. 13.
8. ibid., p. 13.
9. ibid., p. 14.
10. L. S. Thornton, 'The Meaning of Christian Sociology', *Christendom*, 1:1, 1931, p. 26.
11. Williams, 'Liberation Theology and the Anglican Tradition', p. 14.
12. ibid., p. 15.
13. ibid., p. 17.
14. Nicholls, 'Two Tendencies in Anglo-Catholic Political Theology', p. 30.
15. ibid., pp. 33–4.
16. Williams, 'Liberation Theology and the Anglican Tradition', p. 22.
17. ibid., p. 22.
18. ibid., p. 23.
19. Rowan Williams, 'Poverty' (Jubilee Group, 1987), p. 12.
20. Rowan Williams, *Bevan Foundation Review*, Issue 1, Autumn 2002, p. 42.
21. ibid., p. 42.
22. ibid., p. 42.
23. Rowan Williams, 'The Kingdom is Theirs' (CSM), p. 7.
24. John Kennedy, 'Ethics and Wealth Creation', *Epworth Review*, September 1993, p. 66 ff.
25. John Kennedy, 'The Wolf, the Goat and the Lettuce: The Church and the European Model of Political Economy' in *God and the Marketplace: Essays on the Morality of Wealth Creation* (IEA Health and Welfare Unit, 1993), p. 83 ff.
26. ibid., pp. 88–9.
27. Kennedy, 'Ethics and Wealth Creation', p. 74.
28. Kennedy, 'The Wolf, the Goat and the Lettuce', p. 107.
29. The lecture is available online at www.anglocatholicsocialism.org.

Index of Names